YOU OUGHTA BE IN BU$INESS

The Humorous Guide fot the Self-Employed

Michael Pilla

YOU OUGHTA BE IN BUSINESS

The Humorous Guide fot the Self-Employed

Michael Pilla

ISBN-13: 978-1-957351-38-4

Published by Nico 11 Publishing & Design
Mukwonago, Wisconsin
www.nico11publishing.com
Quantity order requests can be emailed to:
mike@nico11publishing.com

Be well read.

You Oughta Be In Business
The Humorous Guide for the Self-Employed
2nd Edition

Author: Michael Pilla
Contributing Editor: Michael Nicloy
Interior Layout: Michael Pilla, Griffin Mill
Cover Design: Michael Pilla

Michael Pilla

To Debra
Now and forever, my one and only.

Before we begin . . .

A budding entrepreneur falls into a hole on the way to an important meeting (with these sorts of stories, it never pays to ask how or why), and frantically calls out for help.

A tech billionaire passes by and hears the cries, "Whoa, dude, what are you doing down there?" "I really don't know, can you help me?" "Sure. I'll Venmo you some cash, and you can buy your way out. What's your handle?" The billionaire takes out a smartphone, transfers the funds, and moves on. "Wait, pleads the entrepreneur, the reception here is really bad, and I can't tell if thetransaction went through…"

A Shaman passes by and hears the cries, "My goodness, how did you ever get yourself into such a terrible situation?" "I really don't know, can you help me?" "Why, of course," the Shaman starts to pray. "Great Spirit who lives within us all, please fill this soul with your love so they may walk among us again." Pleased, the Shaman smiles, nods, and moves on. "Thanks, I feel a lot better, but I'm still stuck down here…"

A third person passes by, hears the cries, and immediately jumps into the hole. "Why'd you do that for? Now we're both stuck down here."

"Don't worry," the third passerby said reassuringly, " I've been down here before. I know the way out!"

You Oughta Be In Business

INTRODUCTION

Two neighboring entrepreneurs are getting their shipments of office supplies from Amazon.
As they come out to collect their boxes, the delivery man notices that the first one is all pulled together with the right shoes, jacket, briefcase, and

haircut—a veritable business icon. The second one can barely stay awake and has turned "the wrinkle" into a personal fashion statement.

The driver, being the friendly sort who one often finds delivering such packages, strikes up a conversation with Entrepreneur #1.

"So, how's business?" he asks.

"Great. I have everything in place: my lawyer, an accountant, a business plan . . . a pen with my company name on it that also shoots mace. Here, have one. Now all I need are some clients. Are you happy with your 401K?"

The Driver smiles and politely turns his attention to Entrepreneur #2. "So, how's business?" he asks.

"Huh?" the sleep-deprived, embryonic Captain of Industry replies. "Ah, great, I guess.

Since I went out on my own, I've been so busy that work seems to be the only thing I have time for—never been busier. But, hey, I got to run."

Whom would you say is off to a better start? The entrepreneur who set up everything by the book or the one who jumped in and started doing business.

I started my company almost three decades ago, on Columbus Day. Then, entrepreneurship wasn't as trendy as it is today. Like the Great Navigator before me, I was heading into uncharted waters with only a dream, a MAC PC, a used card table, and a mild sense of desperation.

There were, and are, plenty of books about starting and running a small business. Unfortunately, most of them take a "top-down" approach, written by former corporate executives with seed money and an extensive list of connections and cronies. They deal with such issues as Team Building, creating a Succession Plan, Shredding Documents, and the other "requirements" of starting a company.

But what if you're starting from scratch, with only your wits to count on? How do you deal with the day-to-day, real-world, in-your-face issues you'll face? How do you avoid getting mired in the endless minutia that goes into setting up a budding enterprise? How will you find clients? How will they find you? Where will you work? How do you manage your time? What kind of coffee "system" should you buy? A traditional drip pot or the one with all the little pods? Where do all those pods end up?

Whether you're using your inheritance to develop an App to avoid running into former lovers or you're a laid-off financial professional with a sudden passion for installing central air conditioning, there are issues, problems, and sources of aggravation that are common to any small business owner, things that are considered beneath the notice of Business Books or in Business Schools. (I'll bet you no Professor at Wharton ever suggested you hire your pets.)

Running your own business is not for everybody. You are the most demanding boss you will ever have. You will continually make yourself do things that would send you running to a labor lawyer had you been working for anyone else. You will keep grueling hours, shouldering soul-crushing responsibilities, and seriously question your sanity.

But it could also be the best job you'll ever have.

Your adventure begins...

Chapter 1:
Entreprenurial
Profiles

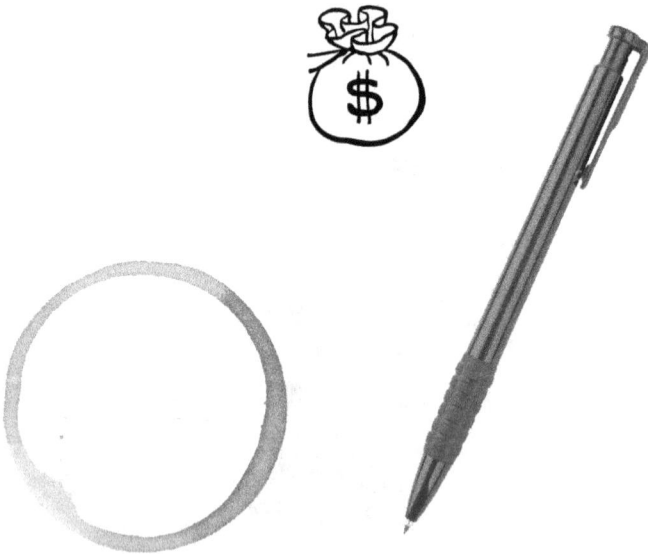

The Many Reasons for Taking the Leap

What would cause a seemingly stable person, with no obvious masochistic tendencies or visible means of support, to leave the relative stability of the nine-to-five world and say, "WTF, I'm taking a chance on me!

Small businesses are often heralded as the backbone of the American economy—the engine of job creation. Yet, ironically many people start a business because they can't find a job in the first place.

Entrepreneurs come in all shapes, sizes, and levels of bravado, but there are basically five reasons why someone might decide to "take the leap" and invest in themselves.

Reason #1:
Downsizing

"Would you please come into the conference room... and close the door."

My personal journey to the land of entrepreneurship started with an innocent request to come in early the following morning for a "special meeting." I quickly discovered just how "special" special could be—I was led directly into the conference room only to be told that this great new company that I'd only been working with for a total of EIGHT WEEKS had come to the sudden realization that they had NO CLIENTS, so here is your severance pay and would you PLEASE clean out your desk and quietly leave within the hour, so as not to alarm the remaining employees whom we will get around to sacking in a couple of weeks.

I got laid off.

I had the Jean-Paul Sartre "No Exit" Package and faced a long and uncertain job search.

At that point, I had had enough of corporate life, it was the third time I was forced out in the last eighteen months, and I decided to seize this opportunity to hire myself—since it is marginally better in the eyes of the world to be "self" rather than "un'" employed—and if anybody were ever to fire me again, it would be me.

Go ahead and give in to the urge to show your former employers what a bunch of short-sighted losers they are. As I learned from my Sicilian Grandmother, spite can be a powerful motivator. (She lived to be 94.)

There is the added satisfaction of knowing that if your former employer is doing as badly as they appear, you will be in business longer than they will.

Reason #2:
Invisibility

"Oh really, you've been working here that long?!"

Has the top of your head been flattened from banging up against that cement ceiling? Is the buzzing sound you hear that of colleagues whizzing by you up the company ladder? Does your boss regularly ask you to take the new guy or gal "under your wing" because the company has big plans—for THEM?

You might do what you do so well that you've been taken for granted—along with the water cooler and the Ficus plant, you are part of the furniture. Invisible until someone higher up needs a favor.

It's time to shake things up and take your talents on the road.

Give yourself the opportunity to try new things, meet new people, and reassess where you are now and where you'd like to be. You might even decide to take another full-time job, but you'll do so with a fresh perspective.

Then there is also a matter of respect. With your employer, you may only be that funny little guy with a beard who works in sales. With your clients, you are the guru, the Thought Leader, the Go To man or woman—your every utterance is a precious gem; every insight received with awe; your contributions are indispensable. Your participation is vital to the project's success and, by extension, the company.

YOU are now The Outside Consultant!!!

Reason #3:
Momentum

"I'll meet you after work in the back of that café on Tenth Street, ask for Mr. Pink, bring cash."

Depending on what you do for a living, you might have picked up a few freelance projects during the course of your career. Slowly (or not, as the case may be), one project becomes three, three becomes five, and suddenly you're working nights, weekends, and holidays.

You're running a covert operation, a clandestine freelance business. Lunch hours are for hurried business meetings, nights and weekends are for completing the extra assignments, off-hour Zoom meetings, and secret strategy sessions in out-of-the- way parking lots under an assumed name.

You're running out of imaginative excuses to cover your many absences. Your sleeping habits have become so erratic that the dark circles under your eyes have you looking like a raccoon, and your harried, dazed, and disoriented demeanor has your boss convinced you might be a zombie. In other words, your full-time job is interfering with your freelance work.

Leave the entrepreneurial closet and stop living this double life.

Despite the damage to your health and any relationship you might be in, there are many advantages to this scenario:

• You'll be drawing a regular salary as you start building your business,

• You can afford to pick and choose your assignments

• You'll have an active client list to ease your transition.

• Best of all, if you've put away some of that freelance dough, you can self-finance your self-employment, negating the need for banks, family money, and loan sharks.

Reason #4:
The Vision Thing

"Eureka, Goddamit."

Are you the kind of person who has their own way of doing things, who can look at an everyday object and say, "If we put this over there and add that thing, we could really have something."

One night, deep in REM sleep, your mind awash with the mental bric-a-brac of the day welling up from your unconscious when... Sudenly awake, you scramble to frantically get your thoughts on paper before the inspiration fades away— like a bolt of lightning, you have been hit by THE BIG IDEA.

You are in the vice-like grip of sudden inspiration. It's The Next Big Thing, The Game Changer, A Thing that Does Something Faster/Cheaper/Better than That Other Thing Ever Did. Hyper-focused, you spend the next several days, nights, or even years, breathing, eating, and sleeping (or not sleeping) the realization of your vision. Your life becomes all about The Big Idea (TBI!)

This is self-employment on steroids.

People who get their TBI to pay off are the rock stars of small businesses. The Miracle Mop, The Walt Disney Company, Spanx, Amazon, Apple Computer, and the iThings started as inspirations from their Messianic founders. They are passionate, focused, obsessed, and, at times, incredibly irritating to be around. Ironically, many VISIONARIES fail to SEE just how difficult they are to work with.

If this sounds like you, give it a shot. Most revolutionary ideas started off the grid in somebody's garage (One day, a President will create a Secretary of Garages to spur economic growth). You'll never know if your good idea is great or a dud if you don't take it out for a spin.

BUT BE WARNED: You risk being either a huge success or a complete waste of time. Go ahead and Google Elizabeth Holmes and Theranos, We Work, Pets.com, or Quibi to see what I mean.

Reason #5:
Your Time has come

"I'm calling my own shots—finally."

After spending a decades career working for someone else, maybe you decided to cash out along and retire. Or maybe, after reaching a hitherto unmentioned retirement age, you've been asked to leave by your newly minted 25-year-old manager to make room for younger, fresher ideas that will earn less than you did.

After a respectful interval, you may decide to give it a go and try working for yourself.

You are not alone. A 2022 report by The American Association of Retired Persons (AARP) found that roughly 1.7 million retired Americans just over 3% of total retired Americans, returned to work. Retirees between the ages of 55 and 64 (13%) and between the ages of 65 and 74 (6%) started new businesses in 2019, according to the Global Entrepreneurship Monitor. There are several reasons:

• In general, people are living longer, so they may be "retired" for decades, increasing their "earning years."

• There's only so much puttering around the house, doing chores, traveling and watching the grandkids you can do before you start trolling LinkedIn for another job.

• Seniors have a lifetime's worth of knowledge and still have the desire to contribute to society and put the knowledge to work.

• Income from Social Security and pension payments provide a safety net, so you can be more selective in the work you take on.

You could continue in the same line of work, only this time, you get to do it your way. You can take a hobby that you are passionate about and turn it into a money-making enterprise. You can sign up for some courses and work in a different industry you have always been interested in.

QUIZ

Are You Ready to Take the Leap?

Check all that apply:

___ At least once a week, you have to say, "Thanks, but I've been working here for five years."

___ You're paying the janitor a monthly fee to use his closet to call freelance clients.

___ You will only talk to people who are potential investors.

___ You're asked to show the "New Kid" everything you know before the next pay period.

___ You discover that you are no longer eligible for employee of the week.

___ You spend all week preparing a major report, and your intern gets all the credit— and a job offer— with an office bigger than yours.

___ For the fourth time in the last three months, you tell your supervisor that you're not coming in because you're having a colonoscopy.

___ You categorize coffee shops by their suitability for business meetings.

___ You get up to get a cup of coffee and return to your desk to find your co-workers fighting over your possessions.

___ Your department has been reorganized, renamed, repurposed, and moved to another part of the country, and you never get the memo.

___ You seriously look into buying real estate on Mars.

Chapter 2:

The Rites of Passage

The Journey from Newbie to CEO of You

Starting your own business has many financial ramifications, but switching to working for oneself is also a "Life Changing Event," and like any other L.C.E., becoming our own boss has some psychological consequences. Polling a random group of entrepreneurs found hanging around a local Starbucks waiting for their big breaks, I identified the following phases:

Euphoria, Denial, Panic, Bargaining, Acceptance, Billing

These states may lead to some erratic behavior, and duration times vary from individual to individual. None of them are inherently life-threatening, provided you don't aggravate those around you to the point where they want to put you, and themselves, out of your misery.

Euphoria

Stage One symptoms are immediately apparent after you've "cut the cord," as it were. Depending on your reasons, you may hear yourself saying things like: "I'll never have to work for anyone else again," or "Finally, I can do things my way," or the ever-popular, "Who needed those bozos, anyway."

Visions of afternoons off, four-day work weeks, and never having to put up with office politics again dance through your blog or podcast. (Wow! You'll now have time to have your own pocast!) You're the captain of your ship, the CEO of You, and your own personal hero as you set actualizing your potential. You can't stop gazing at your business cards.

Denial

You refuse to alter your lifestyle in any way to match your new circumstances. You still keep regular work hours, buy extra-large soy half-caf lattes with a dash of Moroccan cinnamon, and drive a gas-guzzling SUV. But underneath it all, hairline fractures appear in your confident façade, and little voices in the back of your head start whispering words like Defaulting, Bankruptcy, Destitution, and, worst of all, Failure. (Funny how those little voices didn't say anything BEFORE you abandoned a steady income.) Later, louder voices, usually belonging to a parent or spouse, will point out that you no longer have any health insurance.

Panic

OH MY GOD!!! I DON'T HAVE A JOB, OH MY GOD!!! I DON'T HAVE A JOB, OH MY GOD!!! I DON'T HAVE A JOB...

Remember to exhale

OH MY GOD!!! I DON'T HAVE A JOB, OH MY GOD!!! I DON'T HAVE A JOB, OH MY GOD!!! I DON'T HAVE A JOB!!!! NO JOB!!!! NO JOB!!!! NO JOB!!!! NO JOB!!!!

This Stage usually lasts somewhere between two seconds and forever. It's at this point that many people get cold feet, chuck the whole idea, and start frantically searching LinkedIn and online job sites like Indeed, ZipRecruiter, and Monster. You desperately reconnect with old cronies and long-lost friends (Hi, it's me, Jed, we belonged to the same Cub Scout Troop back in the day), and check out Laundromat bulletin boards hoping to find an opening, any opening, anywhere.

As you're about to reach rock bottom and abandon all hope, you regain your composure and objectively look at your new situation.

Bargaining

Once you stop hyper-ventilating, you begin to take those first few baby steps towards gaining control of your life—which is why you're doing this in the first place, right?

Besides, it's too soon to turn back. You've told all of your friends about your great plans, probably burned a bridge or two, and spent all that money on those great-looking business cards!

You start negotiating with yourself: You'll eat lunch at home when not meeting clients; you'll set up a workspace in the bedroom instead of renting an office; you'll call everyone you've ever met in your life and ask if they can refer any work to you, or at least buy you a hot meal.

Slowly, you get used to your new reality, and you're ready for the first big break.

Acceptance

As those initial changes in behavior slowly take effect, you realize that, though this may not be the entrepreneur's paradise you had in mind, it's not hell either. Yes, you're working more hours, but they are your hours. Yes, each client is another person you have to answer to, but even the worst of them is only one of many. No one person has your fate in their hands. You can choose what assignments you'll accept and have the freedom say "no." Things may be messier than anticipated, but it's your mess. You can clean it up. You are now ready to enter the Promised Land.

Billing

It happens almost without notice. You keep working on something until there is no more work to be done. You send out that first invoice. You're flush with feelings of achievement (you finished something!) and anticipation every time you check your Venmo account or go to the mailbox.

Finally, the big day comes. Inside your mailbox is a nondescript envelope addressed to your new company containing your final vindication, the ultimate sign of acceptance, the brass ring at the end of the entrepreneurial rainbow.

It contains THE CHECK!

You have proof in hand that someone is willing to PAY you to do your own thing!

!!!WARNING!!!

This is a very dangerous time. Avoid the temptation to return to your free-spending, pre-entrepreneurial ways. Ignore the urge to pick up the check, fly to Rio, or invest in a Network Marketing franchise. You worked hard for that money. Savor the moment, pat yourself on the back. Later you can do something wild and crazy with it, like pay your electric bill.

Congratulations on successfully making the transition from "Working Stiff" to "CEO of You." Regardless of what happens next, whether you stick with it or take full-time job, become highly successful, or have to move back in with your parents, for one brief shining moment, you took a chance on you!

QUIZ

The Rites of Passage
Match the Stage to the statements below.

A. Euphoria
B. Denial
C. Panic
D. Bargaining
E. Acceptance
F. Billing

___ **1.** You're proud of the fact that you've been working 36 hours straight in your pajamas, subsisting on only coffee, breakfast cereal, and a Fruit Rollup your 5-year-old offered you in pity.

___ **2.** You spend your days in a fetal position fondling your old employee ID card, softly whimpering, "precious . . . my precious," over and over.

___ **3.** You burn your boss in effigy.

___ **4.** You buy an Armani suit, leather briefcase, the latest iPad and iPhone, a Keurig Coffee maker, rent an office, and sit back and wait for the jobs to roll in.

___ **5.** You return the suit and the briefcase, sublet the office space to an import/export company from Uzbekistan, and start an email marketing campaign.

___ **6.** You dress up to check the mail.

Chapter 3:

Getting Organized

First, there are a few things you need to get into place.

Gone are the days when you could take over an empty storefront, put a handwritten sign in the window, call yourself a Horticultural Therapist, and announce to the world that you're open for business. Once you've decided to "Become the CEO of You," there are legal, financial, and just plain common sense hoops you need to jump through before you can get down to business.

A little work now will save you the trouble of having to pull your paper work together later if you find youself dealing with a bank, the IRS or any of the many shady buinsess people you may come across.

Any number of books and organizations that are only a Google search away can supply you with the details, but the following outline is an excellent place to start.

Get a Business Idea

One does not "going into business." One decides to "go into a specific type of business." But which one is the right one? There are traditionally three ways to find the biz for you.

Find a problem you can solve, or at least pretend to.

Consultants often refer to these opportunuties as "Pain Points." This is overly dramatic. Issues that rise to the level of "pain" usually require legal expertise, medical attention, or intense dry cleaning. Providing a necessary service, like being a Personal Shopper, is more along the line of "filling a need."

Businesses that fill a need are more stable, easier to manage, and have a built in pipeline of repeat customers and referrals. They include professional services like lawyers, trades such as plumbers and boutiques which offer cosmetics or gift baskets.

But, "filling a need" may not be enough for you. We all will need those little plastic tips at the end of shoelaces called Aglets. If you aspire to be the "Aglets Whisperer," go for it. But if that doesn't make your heart race, look elsewhere.

Turn a passion into something you can charge for.

Say you like to take photos, make short videos, help people with their tax returns, cook gourmet meals, spend your weekends practicing taxidermy—or some combination thereof. These can all be turned into a full-time business or the now trendier "Side hustle."

Nothing comes to mind?

Here's a short list of businesses you can start with little or no money. With your laptop, or tablet and smartphone you can do most of them from your home or anywhere.

Freelance Services: Writing, graphic design, photography, videography, social media management, or be a apid influencer. Nudge friends and family for opportunities and expand your network through online marketplaces like Upwork or Fiverr.

Sell Products Online: Resell other people's products from local retailers or from overseas. If you're "crafty," stop giving away those tea cozies on the holidays and put those knitted babies to work on platforms like Amazon, Etsy, or eBay.

Consultancy Services: If you enjoy telling people what to do, and have expertise in a particular field, you can stop annoying your friends and relatives by selling your services as a consultant in such areas as marketing, human resources, financial management, social media.

Content Creation: Create and sell digital products, such as ebooks, courses, photos, printables, or that new artworld sensation NFT's (Non-Fungible-Tokens.

NFT are any kind of digial asset that cannot be copied but can be sold, bought, raded, or riduculed by your friends. Google NFT's for more info. Let me know what you find out.

Virtual assistance: Offer administrative or technical support services to businesses and other entrepreneurs, working remotely from your computer.

Still at a loss as to what to do? There's always Dog Walking.

Give Your Business a Name

You can only call it "That Thing I Do For Money" for so long. There are three ways to select a name for your business:

Use the name or names of principal partners. Just like Law firms, Accounting Firms, Ad Agencies, and other professional services.

Use your name in conjunction with a product or service. This would personally connect you with your brand, as in The Ford Motor Company, Franks Red Hot Sauce, or Dalton's Dog Food Tasting Service.

Use a name that doesn't make any sense. Through usage, it becomes associated with your brand/product/service, such as Google, Apple, Amazon and Starbucks.

Then there's "Murder, Incorporated." One of the more successful business names was coined by a crime reporter for the New York World Telegraph. The name succinctly describes the service provided, while the "Incorporated" designation assures the buyer that this was a professional, credible, and dependable organization.

Give Your Business a Plan

So, you figured out what what business you're in and given it a name. Just how are you going to make this happen? More to the point, how will you convince others that you can make it happen? Specifically, customers, creditors, banks, skeptical spouses and in-laws?

The answer is your Business Plan!

Your business plan, as the name implies, is a document that provides the basic details about your embryonic enterprise. The Plan outlines your strategy, marketing, operations, finances, and other pertinent information.

Planning Your Business Plan

Countless books, seminars, workshops, websites and coffee klatches have been conducted about "How to Write a Business Plan." To get you started, I offer the following simplified Table of Contents.

- Executive Summary: The short version if you're in a hurry
- Company Description: Just who are you, anyway?
- Market Analysis: What need do you fill. Who else fills it?
- Management and Staff: Even if it's just you. If you want to look bigger, include the names of friends, family members, and pets.
- Service or Product Line: Just what the hell are you doing, anyway
- Marketing & Sales: How are you going to spread the word
- Funding Request: Buddy, can you spare $50K…
- Financial Projections: As if…

However, none of those may apply if you start working in your bathrobe. With a freelance, part-time, stay-at-home gig, spending time fiddling with your organizational flow chart or succession plan may be a premature. You want to be sure that this is something you can, and want, to do over the long haul.

Start with a simple plan and attainable goals, and keep track of your progress, or lack thereof, as the case may be. After three to six months, you'll have a track record, hopefully, a client/customer or two, a few bucks in the bank, and an idea if this is something you want to stick with. At that point, you'll have some real-world experience and practical information to base your plan on.

Or you can jump in "Fake it Until you Make it. Many successful Business Plans should have started with the words "Once upon a time...."

Register Your Business

You must register your business in your home State so the authorities recognize it as a legal entity, allowing you to collect money for your product or services, lease or buy office space, open a bank account, hire help, and even issue stock.

If it's just you the simplest classification is a Sole Proprietorship. You can use your social security number so you cannot separate your business and personal assets. Should you get sued, everything you own is up for grabs. This could also make it hard to get a buisness loan or establish credit for your business

With a LLC (Limited Liability Corporation) you need to apply to the IRS for a EIN, Employee Identification Number. It allows you to separate your personal and business assets offering you more protection from the inevitable unhappy client or deadbeat vendor, . There also various levels of Incorporation you can wade through.

If none of this makes sense, don't listen to me. Please seek advice.

Protect Your Business

Once you've finished all the paperwork, take your newly minted business certficate and open a bank account in your business's name. This will allow you to cash checks, deposit money, etc. If you're running a "cash-only business," good luck hiding from the IRS.

Even if you intend to manage your money entirely online using Apps such as PayPal, Venmo, Zillow, QuickBooks, Mint, or Wave, It pays to open an account with a brick and mortar bank. All banks offer online services, and many of them connect to the apps I just mentioned. Most importantly, it will give you someone to run to for help should the App you depend on crashes, disappears, or gets sold to a Russian Oligarch.

Get an Accountant

The last thing you want to do is run afoul of the IRS. Accountants will help you establish a bookkeeping system, a plan for handling your tax obligations and even argue your case with the tax authorities should there be a "misunderstanding."

Get a Lawyer

Regardless of the size of your business, there will come a time when someone won't be happy with either you or your services and either flat-out refuses to pay you or, worse, threatens to sue you. You'll need some legal muscle to get their attention.

Get a Copyright Attorney

Claim ownership and protect your intellectual assets—your trademark name and logo. Initially, placing a small "TM" after your name/logo is a good stop-gap measure. Eventually, you should register your name with the Federal Government—which involves something of a process. Again, seek advice.

Funding Your Business

As one cannot make things grow without fertilizer, one cannot start or run a business without funding. Before you go any further, you must have some idea of how you are going to pay for the things you need to get started and keep your enterprise afloat until you can develop a regular revenue stream.

I was fortunate enough to have a successful freelance business (now referred to as the trendier "Side Hustle" because nothing says success better than sounding like a drug dealer) while I was still working a full-time job. This allowed me to put money away and purchase some necessary equipment before I "officially" opened the metaphorical doors to my company.

Other less strenuous options are borrowing money from a relative, friend, or bank. Proving that you have a successful Side Hustle makes it easier to secure a bank loan since you now have a track record you can point to, which in most cases is better than getting down on your knees and pleading with the loan officer.

Promote Your Business

Having the best business idea in the world with a snappy name, all the legal documents filled out, and a bushel of money is useless if no one knows you exist. You will need to find clients, and they will need find you. You will have to get the word out!

The first step is to do some basic market research to understand your business environment. In other words:

- What exactly are you offering?
- Why should anyone care?
- Who needs what you are selling?
- Will anybody buy what you are selling?
- Who are these anybodies?
- Will those anybodies buy from you or somebody else?
- Is there enough business for you and all those other somebodies?

Take the information you gathered during your market reserach and create, or get someone who knows what they are doing to create, the following basic items:

Business Card

Believe it or not with all the technological advances in communications during the last 100 years, business cards are still one of the most effective ways of promoting yourself.

Think of it as a combination of it as a mini billboard and party invitation. Hand them out at networking events, parties, meetings, and random moments when you run into someone who needs your services so you're not continually scribbling your name and number on odd bits of paper every time you meet a prospect.

We also now have the virtual business card that lives in your smartphone. It allows you to instantly transfer your contact information into your prospect's phone. Once there, the information is clickable, so your phone number and website are one touch away.

Website

The other crucial requirement is a website. You can put up a basic but usable one using either Six or Squarespace. They both come with a larger number of pre-existing templates and other built-in features, so you don't have to be Bill Gates. The website will give Google something to find if prospects go looking for you.

A Social Media

presence is also a good idea. I recommend you start with LinkedIn, because it's all business, and Facebook, because, despite Mark Zuckerberg's P.R. problems, it still has approximately 3 billion members. At least a few of them will want what you are selling, plus its advertising is still a great value and incredibly targeted.

With all this in place you're almost ready to start...

QUIZ

Getting your ducks in a row.
Choose the correct answer:

1.The first thing you need to do when starting a business is:
A) Sit down with a cold drink until you come to your senses
B) Buy snappy business cards so you don't look like a "newbie"
C) Decide what kind of business you want to have
D) Quit your day job

2.When naming your business, you should
A) Consult a baby naming book
B) Call it "The Thing I Do for Money" until you think of something better.
C) Use your name or one that describes what you do
D) Revise an existing name: FRED EX, Zapple Computer, or StarKlucks

3.Why do you need a Business Plan?
A)I don't know, I was going to ask you.
B) Because the banks don't lend money to businesses that "Wing it"
C) It gives you a blueprint for running and growing your business
D) It will keep you busy until you get clients

4.Why should you protect your new business?
A) Because it's very young and naive and easily fooled
B) Because people suck
C) Because you want to keep your hard-won assets safe
D) Because your brother is a lawyer and needs the work

5.Once you have all the paperwork in place, you should
A) Take a short vacation. That was a lot of work
B) Wait patiently for the inevitable rush of clients
C) Get the word out any way you can
D) Reconsider before it's too late

Chapter 4:

Your Workspace

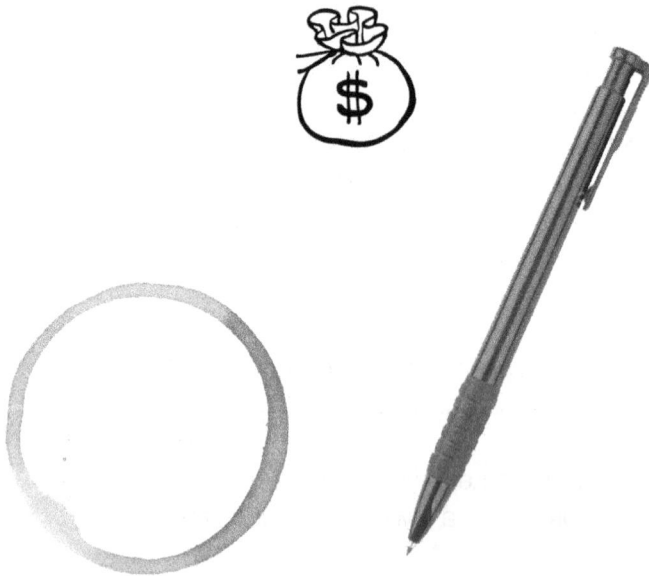

The Next Normal: Working by remote control

After nailing down he nature of your business, the next important item on your to do list should be where are you going to get your work done?

Since the Covid-19 Pandemic and the resulting lockdown from March of 2020 to the end of 2021, things have changed because they had to. Working from home was no longer a temporary situation, but a necessity. Going to an office, with the crowds, the commuting and the close contact with your associates was potentially dangerous.

As humans have done since standing up in the African savanna, we have adapted our technologies, procedures and ourselves. We adjusted to this "Next Normal" and, though we initlally had no idea of how were going to do it, life went on.

Redefining the Workplace

The deadly airborne virus was spread by close contact; you could catch it by breathing close to someone infected. With everybody sheltering in place and keeping six feet apart—it was either six feet apart or six feet under—how would any work get done?

Enter Zoom, an easy to use, video conferencing platform

Developed as a cost-saving alternative to flying executives across the globe, it became crucial to business communications for everything from board meetings to presentations to brainstorming sessions.

Was that Zoom Good for you? Zoom Ettiqutet

Zoom not only introduces a new way of doing business but also creates a different way of interacting with fellow human beings. As with any social environment, there need to be rules of decorum to ensure a satisfying Zoom experience for all. Just follow these simple rules:

#1 For Pete's Sake, Get Fully Dressed—Avoid the temptation only to dress up the parts that show. It is almost impossible to keep your head in the game when you are wearing professional business attire from the waist up and pajamas with fuzzy slippers, or less, below the belt.

#2 Create Zoom Room —Set yourself up in a quiet space in your home, office, or home office where you will not be disturbed, and your call will not disturb anyone else. Be mindful of your background. If you are working from home, you might not want clients to see an unmade bed. Plenty of real and virtual environments are available online, so you can look like you're Zooming from Paris when you are in your basement.

#3 Keep the Video On—No hiding Behind the Black Screen
This side of the witness protection program, I find it off-putting to address a black screen showing only a name in white letters. Aside from being rude, it's distracting. Just what is going on back there? What is it you don't want me to see? Your office? Your home? Did you forget to get dressed?

#4 Put the iPhone Down and Pay Attention—Stay focused on the meeting and what others are saying. In a Zoom group, your mind might begin, and you start checking your phone, talking to someone off-screen, or even eating. If you must munch on a cookie, or a carrot stick for that matter, please mute yourself so the crunchy sound of you chewing does not disrupt the meeting.

#5 Plan Your Zoom, and Zoom Your Plan—The medium might be new, but a Zoom meeting is still a meeting. Prepare the agenda and any notes or relevant information beforehand and email them to the attendees so that everyone is clear on the purpose of the meeting and they can participate. Allow screen sharing for presentations, and encourage them to share contact information and links in the Chat. You can record the proceedings should you need to take notes later.

When the "Home Office" is a "Home Office."

As restrictions gradually loosened up, workers and entrepreneurs now wondered if they even needed an office anymore. Many businesses have adopted flexible hybrid schedules, with employees working part of the week in the traditional office, and part of the week remotely from somewhere else like home, a local Starbucks, or visiting a "client" in Buenos Aries. As long as you had an internet connection and, a laptop or tablet, and a smartphone, geography was irrelevant.

Depending on what business they are in, for entrepreneurs, this represented huge cost savings—no rent or commuting costs— plus, there is no longer any stigma attached to "working from home." They are no longer running a penny-pinching start-up but are now at the cutting edge of making a living…or whatever.

As I have stated previously, Zoom and other easy-to-use video conferencing platforms, plus advances in mobile computing, have made working remotely not only possible but, in many instances, preferable!

Over half of Fortune 500 companies reportedly used Zoom in 2019, and during 2020 it hit even greater heights, racking up 227 percent growth over the year. Not surprisingly, Google and Microsoft have come out with their own versions.

Many successful entrepreneurial enterprises have started out in the corner of the living room, in the basement behind the water heater, or in extreme cases, a closet. The price is right, and you'll have the shortest possible commute.

If you can help it, do not put the office in your bedroom if you value your sanity. Nothing is worse than working twenty-two hours straight only to have your work taunting you when you awake from the pitifully few hours of sleep you've been able to squeeze into your schedule.

In some cases, the "home office" isn't a room at all but a piece of furniture that opens up to reveal your desk, a computer, files, and, for some, an assortment of action figures. Whatever arrangement you decide on, constant vigilance will be required to keep your workspace from taking over your living space. The moment you let your guard down, you could find yourself living in what amounts to a file cabinet.

Getting Stuff

The space of any configuration is of little value if it's empty. You'll need to fill it with things so you can get your work done and, of course, get paid.

Computers

During the Pandemic, they became more essential than ever. You already have a home desktop or laptop computer, but now you'll be asking it to do more as your all-in-one communications, networking, production, photo/ video/audio editing, design, writing, storage, and archiving platform.

You most likely aready have a home computer for games. email, ans the occasional movie. Unless you want to experience the joy of having it crash just as you finish that presentation you forgot to save, you should look into upgrading to a more powerful one.

Get a computer with the following attributes:

1. Increased processing power: Ensure your desktop/laptop/ mobile device has enough advanced processing power capable of handling complex tasks and significant amounts of data with incredible speed and efficiency. Intel Core i5 or i7 or AMD Ryzen 5 or 7 are good options. You should also have enough memory.

2. Cloud computing: The rise of cloud computing has enabled businesses to store their data and software in offsite data centers, reducing the need for on-site servers and storage. This has also made it easier for employees to access data and applications from any location and device.

3. Improved security: With the increasing cyber-attack threat, security has become a significant concern for businesses. Advances in cybersecurity technologies, such as advanced firewalls, intrusion detection systems, and encryption technologies, have helped to protect against threats and keep sensitive data safe. Look for a computer with built-in security features such as antivirus software, firewalls, and encryption capabilities. You can add additional security from any number of software vendors.

4. Collaboration and communication tools: Today, all computers come with WiFi installed as remote work, and collaboration has become essential for businesses. Advances in video conferencing, messaging, and project management software have made it easier for teams to communicate and work together from anywhere in the world.

5. Mobile computing: The increasing power and portability of laptops, tablets, and smartphones have enabled employees to work from anywhere at any time. This has led to greater flexibility and productivity in the workplace. Some of these have touchscreens that eliminate the need for a stylus. Others are hybrids between a desktop and a tablet — a docking station allows your tablet to act as a desktop with a separate keyboard.

6. Warranty and Support: Choose a computer from a reputable manufacturer with a good warranty and technical support options in case you need assistance. Apple products have Apple Care ans the Genius Bar at any Apple retail outlet. For other brnads check out the Geek Squad

Making specific recommendations is like picking the winner of Super Bowl LXXX (that's Super Bowl 80 for those of you who did not go to Catholic School). Sure, the Eagles and Chiefs look good now, but the Jacksonville Jaguars might get it together by then, and there goes your retirement fund.

I'm no expert, but after a lot of Googling, at this writing, I would look at Dell, Hewlett Packard (HP), and Microsoft for Laptops; Samsung and Microsoft for Tablets; and Dell and HP for Desktops. I like Apple products across the board (laptops, IPads, Desktops)

Of course, you can do your own Googling, or roll the dice and ask that nice undergrad working at your local computer store for help. Ask several of them and see if you get the same answers.

All-in-One Peripheral

You also already have a printer that also scans and faxes…or at least you should. Again, look into upgrading, as you'll probably be printing a lot more, and in color. If you want the best print qulaiity look into all-in-one- laser printers, but the printer and it's cartridges come at a higher cost.

Going Mobile: Tablets and/or smart phone

These are the best thing to happen to self-employed since tax deductions. Everywhere pedestrians risk getting run over, and people everywhere risk permanent Cervical Spine injury by constantly staring into their phones. In fact, people are so terrified of NOT having their phones that the National Institute of Health has given it a name. NOMOPHOBIA is used to describe a psychological condition when people have a fear of being detached from mobile phone connectivity. A portable power pac will insure that your phone never runs out of power while you're on the go

Beyond email, texting, and selfies, you should configure your virtual business to be mobile-friendly: keep and back up files to the cloud, make sure your website is mobile- friendly, and take advantage of relevant apps—if you're really into it, maybe even get a custom app developed just for you.

Top Business Apps

One way to spend money to save or "make time" is through technology. Technology is a wonderful thing (OK, when it works). Always available, never takes a vacation, endlessly flexible, and no one will ever knock on your door asking about payroll taxes and workman's comp.

There are many job-specific apps, software packages, and third-party platforms (and more coming every day) that you can access on an as-need basis to make your work life more efficient and your life-life easier. Many offer a free seven to thirty-day trial, after which there will be a small monthly fee, but you can cancel your subscription as soon as it's no longer useful.

Some of the more popular third-party platforms are also available as Apps, so you can download them to your mobile device and have them with you everywhere, all the time:

1. Microsoft 365 — With Word, Excel, and PowerPoint all in one app, Microsoft 365 is the destination for creating and editing documents on the fly. – www.microsoft.com/en-us/microsoft-365/what-is-microsoft-365

2. Amazon Web Services — Build, Deploy, and Manage Websites, Apps or Processes on AWS' Secure, Reliable Network. Sign Up for a Free Account - aws.amazon.com/

3. Google Docs —Get access Googles' word processor, spread sheet, and presenttaion software that can all be stored on your Google Drive. Alll online and accessible from anywhere at any time.

4. Slack — If you are working with teams, Slack is an instant messaging program where you can share messages, announcements, documents, audio and video clips and keep everyone on the same page, https://slack.com/

5. Grammarly — A super spellcheck, Grammarly catches spelling, grammar, punctuation, and clarity, errors while allowing users to customize their style, tone, and context-specific language.- https://grammarly.com/

6. Canva — A free-to-use online graphic design tool. Use it to create social media posts, presentations, posters, videos, logos, and more.

7. Trello—A Collaboration/Project Management tool. Trello is a visual tool that empowers your team to manage any type of project, workflow, or task tracking. Add files, checklists, or even automation: Customize it all for how your team works best.

8. Gusto — An innovative payroll software designed to automate and streamline the payroll process for small to medium-sized businesses. With its user-friendly interface and powerful features, Gusto Payroll helps business owners save time, reduce errors, and stay compliant with tax regulations.

9. Wave — Online bookkeeping with lots of free options, Wave allows you to search transactions, design accounting reports and reconcile data across other Wave products. Plus, you can calculate sales tax automatically, customize payment terms and enjoy access to easy-to-understand cash flow insights.

10. Squarespace — An all-in-one content management system, or CMS. With a single subscription, you can make a website, host your content, register your own custom domain name, sell products, track your site's analytics, and much more.

11. Constant Contact —Email marketing software that primarily helps businesses create and track branded emails, websites, online stores and more in one online marketing platform

12. QuickBooks — QuickBooks is a user-friendly, simple accounting software that tracks your business income and expenses, and organises your financial information for you, eliminating manual data entry.

You will also need...

A Coffee Machine

Next to an accountant with a whimsical interpretation of the tax code, your best friend will be your coffee machine. It will be there to help you toast victory, it will be there to console you in defeat, and it will be there to get you through the long days and nights that running your biz requires.

Get a regular coffee maker. You won't have time to clean a fancy cappuccino machine. You can also get a "Coffee System" with pre-measured coffee in little plastic pods so that you won't have to deal with coffee grounds. They also make tea and hot chocolate, so you'll have some Barista training should you need extra cash.

Basic Office Supplies

Do not overlook the obvious. I cannot tell you how much time I have wasted looking for a pen, rummaging through files looking for a paperclip to reuse, or cursing at an empty tape dispenser. Running out of paper for the printer or having an ink cartridge run dry at 2 AM is fun too. With all the time we spend online, it's easy to forget that not everything is virtual—always buy more than you need and stock up!

Moving Out and Moving Up

If things are going well and you are relatively sure that you have a viable business, there'll come a time when you'll want to stop being an entrepreneurial shut-in and actually leave the house. Again, you have several options:

Temporary Office Suites

Think of them as functioning like an Office Hotel with rooms and cubicles that can be leased to solopreneurs and that small businesses lease on a monthly basis. The concept has been expanded, with some Suites offering workshops, after-work activities, popcorn machines, and other features designed to make the workplace feel more like a community. In some cases, these places act as incubators, creating an environment that encourages individual small businesses to come together and hatch something bigger.

They will also answer your phone, take messages and give you a prestigious-sounding mailing address. Many provide support/ secretarial services should you have the sudden urge to get something collated.

If you're tired of having client meetings in diners, they can also provide you with a conference room so you can look like a grown-up when you have to.

The Major Leagues: Leasing Your Own Space

If things are going REALLY well, you might be able to rent an office of your own! If you're doing really well, then YOU could lease more space than you need and rent out the extra office space to other entrepreneurs, thus continuing the circle of life.

Other considerations:

Your Car

While I don't recommend working from your car, if you live in a suburban area, you'll spend so much time behind the wheel that you might think of it as a second office (or as your own Mobile Business Vehicle). It's not a bad idea to keep some basic emergency supplies in the trunk: presentation folders, pens, pads, a stapler, batteries, antacids, and other items that relate to your business.

If your car is essential to your business, it will be in your best interest to:

• Keep it in good running order and

• Stay on the good side of your local Motor Vehicle Bureau. Nothing will disrupt your week faster than getting towed for unpaid parking tickets and running out to the pound to retrieve your auto—or so I've heard.

QUIZ

Setting up your workspace in your home or office
Mark the statements True or False

____ Spend as much money as you can on office space to impress your clients.

____ To save space, it's a good idea to put the office in the bedroom.

____ The Virtual Office is where you pretend to work.

____ The most important piece of equipment is your coffee maker.

____ When in doubt, work out of your car.

____ Smartphones are the worst thing to happen to entrepreneurs since payroll taxes.

____ The Internet has made the whole concept of office space irrelevant.

____ Working from home has its problems, but you can't beat the commute.

____ Office Suites is a company that makes cupcakes for office parties.

____ Temporary office arrangements are for part-time jobs.

____ Sub-leasing office space is a great way to expand your business while keeping your expenses low.

Chapter 5:

The Four Horsemen

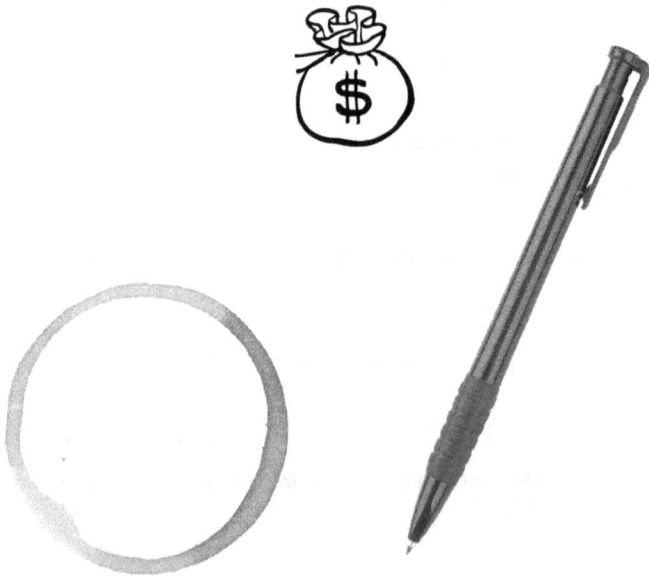

Don't let managing your business get Medieval on you.

While flipping through The Book of Revelation, one day, I came across its predictions for the Apocalypse. According to scripture, The End of the World would be heralded by the arrival of The Four Horsemen: Pestilence, Famine, Destruction, and Death. I don't think about the Apocalypse, though it would take care of that Visa bill.

As I read on and saw parallels between these harbingers of doom and my management issues. Every challenge I faced fell into one of FOUR categories:

> Cash Flow
> Client Acquisition
> Project Management
> Client Relations

If you are plagued with unpaid invoices, a sales process starving for prospects, production schedules that are in shambles, and the fresh hell of difficult clients that you wish would "just go away," read on, oh intrepid warrior.

Reining in your business

Once you decide to go into business for yourself, you will need to shift your perspective. As an employee, you had a specific role in a larger enterprise. But as a business owner, you are responsible for every aspect of your business, and your success will depend on how you run that business.

To be successful, you need to work ON your business instead of IN your business. It may mean putting less emphasis on doing what you do best and devoting a significant amount of time to keeping things running.

Hence my "Four Horsemen," or if you prefer, "Horse Persons."

- **Cash Flow**—Managing your money.
- **Client Acquisitions**—Keeping the clients coming.
- **Project Management**—Keeping the work moving.
- **Client Relations**—Keeping the clients happy.

Just as the original Four Horseman foretold illness, misery, destruction, and the onset of Armageddon. My failure to corral The Four Horseman of Small Business Success foretold no income, unhappy clients, sleepless nights, and the onset of "Arma- get-a-job" before the "End Days" of bankruptcy were upon me.

They represent a fundamental organizing principle, a way to remember the building blocks of managing my business. They allow me to rein in the seemingly endless day-to-day minutia and charge into the entrepreneur's equivalent of the "land of milk and honey."

Plus, I'm a big fan of Medival History.

Each one of these essential business functions warrants a book of their own. For now, I'll give you a brief overview and supply more details, insights, anecdotes, and just plain nuggets of information in the proceeding chapters.

Huzzah!

Horseman #1:
Cash Flow

Regardless of size or industry, cash is the life's blood for every business, and, not unlike your circulatory system, everything comes down to keeping it flowing. With this one under control, you have resources, options, and no reason to hide under the desk when caller ID flashes "Unknown."

Many business books see this as a matter of accounting, of keeping track of income and expenses. They reduce managing cash flow to an exercise in bookkeeping, of adding up neat little columns of figures, subtracting one from the other, and making sure the one marked "IN" is bigger than the one marked "OUT." Avoid buying things you can't afford, and things will be hunky-dory.

This is fine if your business is located in Fantasy Land.

For one thing, you have no income!

You're self-employed, remember?

For another, unless you have an alternate source of cash, a pliable Sugar Daddy, or access to the bank account of an aged but inattentive relative, you'll need money to get your hands on all sorts of things you won't be able to afford. You'll need everything from smartphones to paper clips—and I mean the shiny metal kind, not the expensive multi-colored ones.

You'll have to get creative and think out of the box if you can afford a box since you have to spend it to make it, even though you may not have it. You'll need strategies on how to spend wisely and borrow judiciously if you need to. Too much debt is the Black Knight of small business.

You'll need to work simultaneously on both ends of the income/expense pipeline, spending only what you need on your day-to-day upkeep while putting away what money you can into growing your business, which leads me to Horseman #2.

Horseman #2: Client Acquisition

Thomas Watson, Sr., the founder of IBM, put it best when he said, "Nothing happens until someone makes a sale."

To ensure a steady cash flow, one must continually look for new business. Whatever method you use, acquiring new customers on an ongoing basis, is called your "Sales Pipeline." Right up there with food and oxygen, keeping your Sales Pipeline open, flowing, and unclogged, and by that, I mean continually finding new clients or customers is—WAIT FOR IT—crucial to the survival of your business.

Many somethings have to happen before you make the sale, from selecting your target market to identifying prospects to perfecting your sales pitch to making sure you have the correct address and your socks match before running out to that sales meeting.

There are any number of sales techniques available to you, from the one-on-one intimacy of networking with colleagues to the dizzying array of Digital Marketing platforms to shamelessly sponging off of friends and relations—all designed to get you in front of someone who can write you a check, or Venmo you some cash.

Many start-up owners need help with sales. For some of them it is the biggest barrier to success. They are self-conscious, they feel awkward asking for work, and they have negative associations with sales, equating it with lying or trying to force someone into buying something they don't want.

Call it the used car salesman syndrome.

The key is to think of sales as having a conversation with your prospects. All you are doing is talking about your business and making yourself available.

Whatever sales technique you employ, once you get the work, you're only as good as the job you deliver, which brings us to Horseman #3.

Horseman #3:
Project Management

You went out on your own to do something you love, but now you spend so much time managing the projects that there's little time to practice your craft. If you've worked for a company, there were always people around to spellcheque (see what I mean?), get supplies, make schedules, and so on.

But now, it's also up to you (yes, you!) to see that the whole project is on time, within budget, mistake-free, on target, washed, dressed, pressed, and invoiced. You are the work your company produces; ultimately, you're only as good as your last project.

Welcome to the fun-filled world of Project Management, where you are responsible for the work that other people are, or are not, doing. The sooner you can automate or delegate some or all of these functions—be it to third-party software platforms, Artificial Intelligence, freelance vendors, unpaid relatives, or sometimes, even the client—the better.

Project Management is equal parts art, science, and sweet-talking or threatening people, or even yourself, in order to get the job done. I consider it the most challenging of all the business function out of the four we have here because anything can go wrong at any time, and it's up to you to fix the problem. You are responsible for things you have no control over, among them are schedules, vendors, technology, overnight express companies, and even the weather.

Despite your best efforts, there will always be bumps in the road and times when you have to deliver bad news to the client. At times like that, it helps if you have generated enough goodwill and credibility to get you through the rough spots.

A business relationship is still a relationship and needs to be nurtured in order to be successful. You need to spend some time with Horseman #4.

Horseman #4:
Client Relations

Many entrepreneurs proudly say, "When my clients ask me to jump, I ask how high." They pride themselves on having no pride and place themselves totally at their client's beck and call. They want to be liked!

There are two reasons why this might not be the best approach:

First, you are ceding control of your company, and control is one of the reasons you started this business in the first place. This may make sense if you have only one client who generates so much income that you can be available 24/7 or, of course, if you really like jumping.

Second, this strategy only works if the project proceeds smoothly and the client has a minimum number of psychotic episodes. Once there is a problem, stuff will hit the fan, and you may have to deal with an angry client and a messy fan on top of everything else.

Just as Project Management deals with the physical aspects of the job/project/ assignment, Client Management deals with the emotional roller coaster that is also part of doing business.

You want to be able to guide that relationship and be seen as a professional equal, someone with knowledge and experience in your own right, and not a jumping "Yes" person. Think of yourself as "The Client Whisperer," part therapist, part business partner, and part whatever you do. The Client Whisperer nurtures a feeling of trust, manages the client's expectations, and understands how the client's personality impacts the job at hand.

So there you have them, The Four Horsemen of Small Business: Cash Flow, Client Acquisition, Project Management, and Client Relations. Depending on how you manage them, they can either come riding to your rescue or be the bringers of doom we've all come to know and love.

QUIZ

The Four Horseman of Business Management
Match the Statement to the Horseman

Match the "Horseman" to the statement below:

A. **Cash Flow**
B. **Client Acquisition**
C. **Project Management**
D. **Client Relations**

____ After regaling you with tales of his wealth and success, a potential client asks you to work "pro bono," happily informing you that you will be paid in "karmic" dollars.

____ You might need to replace an online vendor who has been out of touch for over a week when you learn that they are situated in a remote, rural location in Vermont and may have been eaten by bears.

____ Parking tickets, credit cards, vendors, or your mortgage— Eeny, Meeny, Miny, Moe, who's the first to get your dough?

____ Your biggest client has a short temper, a short attention span, and short legs, for that matter. He's an angry little man. You humor him by complimenting his business savvy while pointing out that this week's list of demands will completely undo last week's list of demands.

Chapter 6:

CashFlow

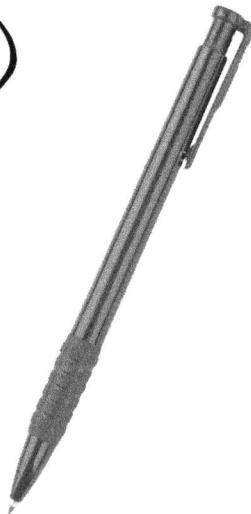

Going with the flow...
or not as the case may be

As I stated earlier, Cash Flow, or Liquidity, if you want to get fancy, is the lifeblood of any business.

Without the benefit of a regular paycheck, your first job is to find ways to keep the cash coming. Your second job is to manage it properly so you'll have enough to keep the doors open and the lights on.

The words "Cash Flow" bring to mind images of a cascading, multi-denominational torrent of twenties, fifties, hundreds, and the odd bit of pocket change, filling you coffers to the brim, making all things possible.

In reality, it can be like trying to fill a leaky bucket with an eye dropper.

A bucket with two spigots.

That's how I visualize Cash Flow—one spigot flowing in and the other flowing out. The one flowing in starts with your clients (assuming you have clients) and the fees you collect. The one flowing out starts with you and flows to your vendors, employees, and the expenses that make it possible for you to do business.

Over the years, I've come across a number of strategies, techniques, and, shall we say, "schemes" to properly manage both faucets and keep enough in the bucket to pay my monthly bills, educate my daughter, and splurge on the occasional Full rack order of BBQ ribs.

Cash Flow: Income

The "IN" faucet starts with your clients. You may not completely control the situation, but ideally, you have set up some sort of a sales pipeline to keep the income heading your way. Here are a few key concepts that have helped me over the years:

Always be on the lookout for new business.

Think of each client as a mini-faucet. The more of these you have, the less likely you are to experience a serious interruption in income. Don't wait until things slow down.

The best advice I ever got was during lunch with an older, grizzled photo re-toucher, "The best time to look for new clients is when you're really busy, kid. You say you don't have the time? Well, you gotta make the time. By the way, you gonna finish that coleslaw?"

His point was that the average period between "Hello, my name is . . ."and putting that first check in the bank is anywhere from three to six months. If I waited until things slowed down to start the process, it could be a while before the new billings started kicking in, and I might be facing the dreaded "cash drought."

Work fast to keep the pipeline moving.

Getting the sale is half the battle. It doesn't do you any good until you can start invoicing. The faster you execute the job, the sooner you can send in the bill. Projects that linger and seem never to end can wind up costing you money in two basic ways:

1. Extra work you are not getting paid for

Now that they've gotten started, the client may want to expand the scope of the project beyond what was originally agreed upon but, of course, insists on the original fee. Many a client will try to bully you into doing the extra work at no cost.

The more devious ones will try to play on your sympathies. I had one client, a nice little old man who planned corporate events, who would experience a senior moment whenever the words "that's not what we agreed to" came up in the conversation. My business partner at the time, a lovely woman with a big heart, could not say no. Unfortunately, it was almost two years before the project was completed, all but destroying the profit from that job.

2. The Client terminates the project before completion.

I have had a few clients drag their heels to the point where they decide that, since they've lived this long without whatever I was doing for them, maybe they didn't need it in the first place. They canceled the project before it was completed, causing a proportionate dent to my income expectations.

Once you've reached the billing stage, there are things you can do to protect your Cash Flow:

Invoice in stages

Regardless of the size or duration of the assignment, get a deposit and bill the rest in increments. It gives you money in hand and makes it less likely that they will back out of the agreement. If they do, at worst, you're never out more than one installment.

Invoice promptly

Don't let those invoices pile up! You need to submit an invoice to get paid. If you wait 30-60 days to bill and the client takes 30-60 days to pay . . . well, let's say that that bucket can empty in a hurry.

My preferred tactic is what I like to call "Whinny Persistence." I'd call every other day or so and apologize for askig for money: "Look, I'm sorry I have to keep asking. The bank they don't understand, they keep asking me for the mortgage payment. I know how hard you must work; if it were up to me, I'd work for free, but the kids . . . they get hungry."

Incorrect Invoice

Another favorite technique is to send an invoice for the wrong amount, add a 1 to the beginning of the number or a zero at the end and wait for the call.

Follow up on late payers.

Collections are the bane of every entrepreneur. In general, the money owed to me has cost me more sleepless nights than the money I owe.

I believe that the Mafia was originally a consortium of businessmen who found themselves spending so much time chasing after late payments that they decided to cut out all that non-profitable "work stuff" and concentrate on making collections.

Whatever technique you use, be sure to stay on top of those open invoices. Talk or send emails to the person directly responsible for cutting the check. With larger companies, you might have better luck with the Accounts Payable person, department, or bookkeeper—it's not their money. For smaller companies or individuals, you'll have to keep at it. As a last resort, tell their mothers.

FINAL NOTE: Don't make the hole any bigger!

Under no circumstances should you do additional work for a client who owes you money, especially one that hints that there is more work around the corner. They probably won't pay for that, either. The absolute worst is the client who tries to blackmail you into doing more work by threatening to withhold money you are already owed. In that case, you have three options: do the work and hope that will be the end of it, take them to court, or walk away and move on to more profitable clients.

Cash Flow: Out go

Now that we've filled the bucket, how do we keep it all from running out the other end? Many entrepreneurs rely on cost control measures, but running a business entails more than just counting beans or stacking pennies.

Don't count your chickens until the check has cleared.

That is, don't spend or plan to spend money you don't have in hand or in the piggy bank or whatever. Many overly optimistic entrepreneurs have hired staff and bought or leased equipment because a client has hinted that more work was on the way. It's best to wait until you have been paid before spending the money.

Keep your overhead low.

The trick here is to reduce costs while still providing quality goods and services. Remember that time IS money; it does you no good to save some bucks if it means taking longer to perform any given task. That time is time you are not spending on more profitable activities.

The two big ticket items are space and people. Avoid renting office space or hiring full-time employees for as long as possible. Once you've made those commitments, they could be hard to get out of, and they will be draining your bank account.

As stated before, thanks to Zoom making it easier to work remorely, you may not even need space.

If you're doing well and you "just need to get out of the house," try subletting or using a shared office set up where they answer the phone, collect your mail, and provide a venue for meetings at an affordable monthly rate. If you do sublet a cubicle somewhere, do not sign any long-term agreements and only work with companies that let you renew or cancel the agreement every thirty days.

As for people, I have two strategies: I try using technology wherever possible, even if it's costly in the short term, and I make use of interns or people who are willing to work for less (or free!) in order to get experience. Stick to freelancers. Only put people on the payroll when you're absolutely sure you can afford them.

Pay your taxes

Regardless of your cash situation, pay your taxes to avoid late fees, penalties and that sick feeling you get when your savings account has been levied. Most of the trouble people get into stems from trying to avoid the whole problem. I know of one person who cannot leave the country because she's afraid of applying for a passport and showing up on the IRS's radar.

Ironically, they can be easy to deal with if you fess up immediately. There was a police show on TV where a detective would advise a newly arrested suspect that "if you come clean with us now, we can help you out, but once you get into the system, it's out of our hands."

Same thing with the. IRS, and State and Local Governments. Come clean early, and they'll work with you, but once you get "into the system," you might be out of options, and that trip to the mailbox can be scary.

Pay credit cards (if you're lucky enough to still have credit)

Keep up with those credit card payments for no other reason than to keep your lines of credit open (think of them as alternate buckets controlled by the forces of darkness).

They can be a very handy safety net (see: "deadbeats" below) and keep you from hitting up your parents —yet again.

Which other bills to pay?

The unspoken, unpleasant truth of running your own business is that there will come a time when you'll have to decide who gets paid this month. When times are tight, only pay the bills you have to pay. But how do you decide? Do you pay the vendor who is crucial to your business or the starving intern who does your proofreading? In comparison, King Solomon had it easy with that baby thing.

While I encourage you all to pay your bills on time, I would prioritize them thusly:

- Never be more than one payment or one month behind
- Pay for your home (mortgage or rent) first
- Taxes would be next, followed by credit cards
- Bills that are charging you interest or a penalty
- Ideally, I like to pay freelancers who are independent contractors and in the same boat I'm in before vendors who are companies; I feel their pain.
- Everybody else

NO CASH NEEDED

So, let's say you need something that you don't have the money for. There are several methods of handling this situation without the risk of incarceration.

No cash needed: Part 1

This technique is sometimes referred to as a "Soft Investment" in business books or "Can you do me a favor? I'm broke" on the street. This one is tricky. Asking people for the occasional favor is one thing, doing it on a regular basis, and you're creeping into "Deadbeat" territory. I've done favors for people with the understanding that the favor will be returned at some later date (yes, just like the opening of Godfather Part I).

You should limit this to small, highly specific activities—proofreading from an editor, cupcakes from a baker, advice on a business issue from a lawyer or accountant, or makeup tips from a paid escort.

Avoid going to the same person more than once unless you can reciprocate. That Deadbeat reputation is hard to live down.

No cash needed: Part 2

Bartering is another popular strategy among entrepreneurs. This can be effective as long as both sides are equally compensated, though, in my experience, one side always feels shortchanged. I once tried bartering design services for workspace, and no matter how much work I did for this guy, he was always annoyed when I worked on my projects for my other clients.

My other experience with bartering was in joining a bartering consortium. Most of the other members were lawyers, and I wound up getting 25 calls from attorneys who wanted something in return for redoing my will.

QUIZ
Choose the Correct Course of Action:

What is Cash Flow?
____ Don't say nothin', must know somethin', just keeps rolling along
____ A bucket with two spigots: one fills the bucket, and the other, usually much bigger, empties it.
____ A simple matter of bookkeeping, subtracting expenses from income and managing what's left over, chuckled the White Rabbit.
____ Something that will be easier to do once you have an income.

What's the best way to collect late payments?
____ You re-submit the invoice adding 50% to get their attention.
____ You casually mention that you have underworld connections.
____ You have your mother call, apologizes for asking for money but, "my son has all these bills and the banks won't leave him alone. Why did he marry that woman? She can't save a penny...
____ You offer to come by and pick up the check.

You just received a large payment. What should you do?
____ Buy yourself something nice.
____ Let the check sit on your desk undeposited, then beg the bank to clear it so your children will have a roof over their heads.
____ Divide it equally between bill paying, savings, and investment.
____ Get it in quarters, spread it out on the bed, and roll around in it.

What does don't count your chickens before they cross the road, mean?
____ Don't do your bookkeeping until your invoices come home to roost
____ Don't plan on spending money before you actually have it in hand.
____ The "chickens" are the work you've been promised, it's best to take a wait and see attitude—thie highway is littered with flat chickens.
____ Unless you're in the poultry business, stay away . . .

Chapter 7:

Client Acquisition

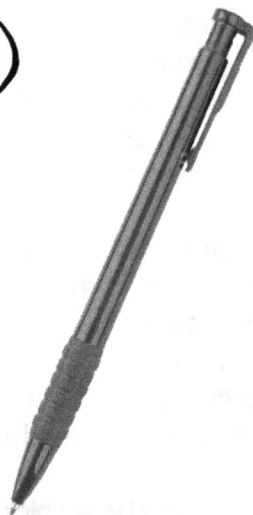

Find new business or you're out of business

Consider the Shark...

Built for speed with a powerful physique and senses so acute that they can detect a frolicking sea lion or a surfer with a paper cut from miles away, all capped off by an endless supply of teeth that can take a bite out of everything from a 1,000-pound tuna to a small marine vessel. All it does is seek, find, and catch its prey. Nature's perpetual hunting/eating machine.

I bring this up because as an entrepreneur, you too need to beconstantly on the prowl for "fresh meat,' or "fresh produce" if you're more of a vegetarian.

But in your case, you're feeding your own kind of primal urge: the need for new business.

The Sales Pipeline

One way to approach finding new business is by establishing a Sales Pipeline. Your Pipeline is a person, place, thing, process, mechanism, or voodoo that allows you to find a steady stream of clients/customers.

Depending on your situation, it could be many things. It could be a partnership with someone in a compatible profession (a Plumber and a Contractor, or a Skydiving School and a Funeral Home), it could be a membership in a professional organization (a trade association or the Cosa Nostra), or it could be an activity on an online platform (LinkedIn or one of those "Chat Rooms").

With a Pipeline, you'll have some idea of where your next juicy piece of business is coming from. Without one, you could be like a sailor in a shipwreck, latching on for dear life to anything that floats by. The trick is not to acquire any old client/customer, but to "attract" the clients who are "right" for you.

Oh sure, you can go out night after night to one white wine/raw vegetable and onion dip-drenched networking event after another and hook up with a string of business owners in tawdry, one-time "quickie" projects, and golly gee, it's fun —for a while.

But then you're left with that empty feeling when they don't call back, and you wind up leaving embarrassing messages like: "Hi, ahhhh . . . it's me. We met at the Small Business Conference. We spent the weekend working on that rush project, and I haven't heard anything from you since. Did you get the invoice I sent you? Guess you're busy . . . anyway, just checking in. I'm here. Call me."

Pathetic.

True happiness is only found in mutual trust, long-term relationships, and repeat business from paying customers. Acquiring such relationships requires a plan— identifying the type of clients you work best with and building your sales strategy and Pipeline around reaching and retaining them while having the discipline to say no.

Keep On Your Toes

Even with a firmly established Pipeline, you never know when or where the next opportunity will present itself—your eyes, ears, and maybe even nose need to be on the lookout.

Be Focused—Clearly define what and whom you're targeting.

Be Prepared—Have a 30-second Elevator Pitch "handy" and ready to go.

Be Attentive — Pounce on the opportunity when it presents itself.

Be Responsive— Keep in touch with your leads until you get a definitive answer. Don't assume they love or hate you until they present you with a signed contract or a restraining order.

Let me give you an example from real life—well my life anyway; the real part is another story.

My wife and I attended a concert by Buckwheat Zydeco at a local performing arts center. Buckwheat popularized "Zydeco" (duh!)—a type of music popular in New Orleans.

Since a recent vacation to New Orleans, we'd been ragin' 'bout anything cajun, so there we were. We bump into a friend my wife had lost touch with, who also just happened to be the venue's, Marketing Director. After the usual round of "You look great!" and "What have you been up to?" Her friend complained that their website has been down since earlier that day, and the developer must also be a magician because he had completely disappeared— no one had heard from him in months.

Turns out, I have a digital marketing firm, and we design and develop—will miracles never cease—websites! I gave her my business card (I never go anywhere without my business cards. I even keep a few in my pajamas), along with my 30-second Pitch. Two weeks later, the site is still down, and I get a semi-frantic call to come in and discuss how I can help. Ultimately I get the contract to redesign/redevelop/rebrand the site.

Fortuitous happenstance aside, it worked out because I was

prepared to jump on the situation BEFORE it presented itself.

Finding New Business

If you're not comfortable relying solely on dumb luck or family connections, there are basically three ways to find new business; or, better yet, have it find you:

Word of Mouth (WOM)—Word-of-mouth advertising has historically been the best and most cost-effective way of getting new business. It opens the door and comes with an implied endorsement from the referrer.

WOM falls into two categories:

Clients of Future Past—Start with your current or former clients. Do a good job; you'll leave a trail of satisfied customers who will happily pass your name along. Like any relationship, these, too, need to be nurtured. Keep them informed about developments in your company.

If they come through, and the referral turns into an actual piece of business, it's usually a good idea to thank them in some small way. Take them to lunch or "do something nice" to re-enforce the human connection and show that you value and appreciate them. A word of caution: "do something nice" usually means a cheeseburger, a nice bottle of wine, or a gift card. If you find yourself having to hand over envelopes of cash (some playfully refer to them as 'kickbacks'), you may want to reconsider the line of work you're in.

Just Plain Folk—Keep in touch with acquaintances, friends, family members, old college buddies, and former lovers, they are also potential sources of referrals. Basically, hound every living creature you know or come across into handing over their address book.

Networking — Another, more professional approach to WOM is to join a Networking Group—a loose association of business people who meet regularly for the purpose of swapping referrals. Usually, these meetings are held weekly, bi-weekly or monthly, and you usually get an opportunity to talk about and promote your business in front of the group.

A side benefit is that it's a great way to refine your elevator pitch. It's like having your own focus group, giving you immediate feedback in a more or less supportive environment. Of course, it would be nice if you could GIVE and GET referrals so as not to sponge off of others' generosity—BNI, LeTip, and others near you are only a Google search away.

Networking Events—Networking Events are a great way to meet new prospects you would never have met any other way. They can be productive and even fun, but it takes discipline and finesse. The idea is to make "First Contact," with the goal of developing relationships that will later result in new business. Don't badger people with your pitch, you'll get further talking about fly fishing than by droning on about your process for determining your clients' projected ROI.

Remember, no one goes to a Networking Event because they have a $25,000 project they're just dying to give away. Most attendees are there to GET work from other attendees. Finding a live prospect in that sea of crudities, white wine, and needy handshakes requires skill. I like Networking Events because I get to see and hear the potential clients—I look for body language and voice inflections—a rarity in today's email, texting, and tweeting business world:

• Does the person seem genuine?
• Can you talk with them easily and potentially establish a rapport?
• Do they need your services?
• Do they live in their car?
• Should they be medicated?
• Do they creep you out?

You'll pick up on a lot in that brief face-to-face meeting that can and will save you lots of time down the road. Collect as many business cards as possible, and follow up by email within 48 hours. Invite them to visit your website or ask them if they'd like to set up a remote meeting, or Zoom call, or meet again in person and continue the conversation.

If they do, you have a live one. If you don't get a response, move on!

Once you've made all those connections, how to keep in touch until they, or someone they know, actually need what you're selling?

Your Online Pipeline

Digital Marketing is a great way to reach new prospects and stay in touch with current clients and contacts. It perfectly complements Networking and all your other new business escapades. The idea is to develop an ongoing online presence, or "footprint," comprised of a website, as many social media platforms as you're comfortable with, an email newsletter, maybe a blog or podcast if you're really ambitious, a smattering of online ads— all giving people and Google, but mostly Google, plenty of ways to keep up with you or find you in the first place.

Keep in mind that your website is the only piece of internet real estate you actually own, is the center of your marketing universe. The other elements—Facebook, LinkedIn, Twitter (now X), Email Marketing, and so on—are there to engage your current contacts, attract new ones, and drive traffic to your site. As with Networking, you are building relationships: be friendly, be generous with information, and be entertaining. The ones who click through to your website are potential clients/customers— people who like what you are putting out and are predisposed to doing business with you.

Cold-Calling: The Rock gets his clients this way—Sales coaches everywhere extoll the virtues of Cold-Calling. Many of them act like drill sergeants and turn this into a test of manhood ("Do you have the stones to make 800 calls a day, maggot?!?"). The implication is that if it's not working, it's because you're not trying hard enough.

It's basically sales by brute force. That said if you find this does work for you, go with God. I would recommend doing what you can to target your calls. Limit yourself to one industry at a time to research and anticipate their needs. Have a script ready so you're not making up the conversation from scratch with each call. Build a list through your referral network so you start out with a relationship in common.

Buying a list of names, numbers, and emails from a broker is always tricky. You don't know if the information is accurate, are the people still in business, or still alive, for that matter. Hire a professional to make the calls and save yourself all that rejection. If only I could have done that when I was dating.

Hire a Salesman—If you have more money than patience, go for it!

Closing the Deal: The Home Stretch—In the film version of David Mamet's Glengarry Glen Ross, Alec Baldwin gives a classic performance as the guy sent by the home office to motivate a rather depressed sales team. To get their attention, he starts by telling a salesman to put down the coffee pot, declaring that "Coffee is for closers." He then proceeds to hammer home his mantra:

"ABC: Always Be Closing."

The point is that you don't want to come up empty after all this effort. The goal is to get the business (and get paid).

Tips for Closing

Success starts with picking the right prospects—As I've said before, don't throw yourself at any potential source of income that comes your way. The fit has to work both ways, and you need to start with some level of rapport. You have to want to do business together.

Listen to their needs—Once you get prospects talking, they will usually tell you what they are looking for and their concerns.

Offer suggestions on how your company can solve their problem. (This of course, assumes that you CAN solve their problem.)

Give them something—Offer some simple advice or a piece of information. Think of it as a free sample. It signals to the prospect that you are willing to deal and not solely interested in separating them from their money.

Follow up— Continue building the relationship. Keep the initial correspondence light and chatty. Stay away from the hard sell, but find a subtle way to re-enforce your sales message.

Submitting a Proposal when asked—and only when asked—Nothing says "God, I need this job," like a blind proposal. Submit it in a timely manner, but give yourself enough time to do a thorough job. Once submitted, follow up to see if they need any further information. Don't let your proposals fall into the prospect's "Bermuda Triangle." Keep in touch until you get a final answer one way or another.

Don't seem needy or desperate.—Remain a professional, especially if you ARE needy and desperate. No one likes a basketcase. Again, no hard sell, but keep them talking.

Know when to back off—The comedian W.C. Fields used to say, "If at first you don't succeed, try, try again. Then give up. There's no use being a damn fool about it." If you're not getting anywhere, move on to more promising prospects.

When the call comes, jump on it—The whole goal of this process is to get the prospect to come to you and make them think it was their idea. When one of them calls wanting to do business, move quickly. Schedule the kick-off meeting, whip up that contract, and agree to any minor concessions; in short, don't let anything stand in the way of closing the deal now that they're ready.

When it's "No thanks, maybe next time," keep in touch—If they choose another company over yours, hang in there and be professional. In the event that your competitor screws up you could get a second chance and the opportunity to play the hero. If not, you might get lucky next time.

QUIZ
Choose the Correct Course of Action:

What is the real job of any entrepreneur?
____ Finding an office
____ Finding clients
____ Finding lunch
____ Finding Nemo

How do you find new clients?
____ Be born into a rich family and mooch off of their connections.
____ Attend networking events and follow the best-dressed people home
____ Whatever works for you, just do it consistenly
____ Beg

What does ABC stand for?
____ Another Bitchy Client
____ Anywhere But China
____ Always Be Closing
____ Anchovies Better Canned

How should you close a deal?
____ Hound them mercilessly until they sign
____ Offer a generous kickback
____ Show them that you can meet their needs
____ Grovel

Chapter 8:

Project Management

Doing what it takes to get the job done

Uncle Johnnie was my family's unofficial baseball coach. Along with learning the finer points of the National Pastime, we also learned life lessons—like thinking ahead. I can still hear him reprimanding one of my cousins for dropping a fly ball after yelling, "I got it, I got it, I got it."

"Now that you got it, what are you going to do with it?" He shouted at the errant fielder.

Indeed, if your client-acquisition efforts have been successful, I would ask you the same question, "Now that you've got the project, what are you going to do with it?"

The disheartening truth about entrepreneurship is that simply getting the work is not enough. I have often been horrified after a particularly productive business development period by realizing that I now had to get all that stuff done! That clients were expecting to see something! Like soon! Like very soon!

The Nagging Art of Project Management.

I have a reoccurring nightmare from my childhood of being this juggler on the Ed Sullivan Show. He would run up and down the stage, balancing a row of spinning plates on sticks. Only in this case, the plates are my workload, the sticks are my vendors, and the frantic music is the clients—or am I the poles, and the plates the clients, and the music representing good intentions?

But I digress.

Many Entrepreneurs initially overlook Project Management. They start as sole practitioners and believe "the work will get done somehow, it always does." Also the words "Project Management" sound so "corporate" since corporations have people called "Project Managers" who spend their days bugging other people until something gets done.

Project Management serves several purposes. It gives you a sense of control over your workflow. It gives the clients the impression that you're on top of things and that their project is in good hands. It also lets you keep all the plates spinning on their sticks.

If you've been paying attention, you've probably guessed by now that over the years, I've developed a number of techniques to keep the assembly line moving while maintaining my sanity.

Avoid Project Creep

No, not the overly needy client with the weird hair who keeps offering you a ride home. I'm referring to the tendency of any project to get bigger before it is completed. This is usually the case with clients driven by "a vision," and the job is less a project and more of a calling; of course, they expect you to believe as they believe, to be more of a disciple then a business associate.

They expect you to go the distance, take it to the next level, do what it takes, take one for the team, and use other euphemisms that basically mean, "can you do more work for less money." I try to

84

humor them as much as possible, but eventually, I have to let them know that I have my own vision that involves paying my bills on time.

Before you start any new project, make sure you and the client are clear on what the job entails. Get it all in writing and have the client sign off. In extreme cases, have them sign in person; in very extreme cases, in front of witnesses. Clearly defined guidelines will ensure that you aren't wasting time. They will allow you to allocate your resources properly and keep any one project from devouring your business.

Develop an Internal Process

No need to reinvent the wheel with every new assignment. There are aspects of most projects that are similar. If you do the same things the same way, time after time, you'll be that much more efficient. I'm in a creative business, and ironically, I've found that having some standardized, boring old procedures in place actually frees me to be more creative! When a new piece of business comes in, I know exactly how I will approach it so I can devote that many more gray cells to finding a unique solution.

Whatever process you develop, keep it simple. The one I came up with has seven steps. I once worked at a place that created a document outlining their process because a major client wanted to know why things took so long. The final version contained 139 individual steps plus various levels of approvals. The client, abandoning all hope of ever seeing anything completed, took their business elsewhere.

Break Your Work into Manageable Chunks

Even while employing your process, things may still seem overwhelming at first, but don't think of the project as an unconquerable whole. As the Chinese Proverb goes: a website of 1000 pages begins as a scribble on a napkin.

Instead of jumping right in, take a step back and develop a plan of action. Approach your assignment as though you were building a house (unless you are building a house, in which case you should think of it as baking a cake.)

Working from the bottom up, identify a sequence of steps or building blocks, give yourself and your team short-term goals, and keep the clients abreast of your progress. Clients get antsy when they haven't heard from you. They start getting visions of you taking their money and spending it on a few days in Cancun.

Set SMART goals: SMART stands for Specific, Measurable, Achievable, Relevant, and Time-bound. It is a simple way to set criteria for your projects and consistenly measure progress:

Specific—Your goal should be clear and focused

Measurable—Quantify the desired results

Achievable—What can you realistically get done

Relevant—The project supports the overall goal

Time-Bound—Give yourself a timeframe.

Create a detailed project plan: Break down your project into smaller tasks, assign responsibilities, and set realistic deadlines. Use project management tools or software to create a visual timeline and track progress.

Communicate effectively: Maintain clear and open communication channels with your team members and stakeholders. Regularly update them on project progress, challenges, and changes. Listen actively and address concerns promptly.

Build a competent team: Select team members with the right skills and expertise for each task. Encourage collaboration and ensure that everyone understands their roles and responsibilities.

Manage risks proactively: Identify potential risks and develop contingency plans. Regularly assess risks throughout the project and take appropriate measures to mitigate them.

Monitor and track progress: Continuously monitor project progress against the plan. Use project management tools to track task completion, milestones, and overall project performance. Regularly review and adjust the plan as needed.

Adapt to changes: Projects often encounter unexpected changes. Be flexible and ready to adapt your plan accordingly. Assess the impact of changes, communicate them to the team and the client.

Allocate Resources

In the military, it's called logistics. It's ensuring the troops have what they need when needed, be it bullets, beans, or Band-Aids. Entrepreneurs need to define their "resources" as broadly as possible: Amazon, Staples, Best Buy, (both online and in-store), downloadable freeware, friends who are between jobs, children home from school, and other people's work.

Before you start, try matching up what you need to do with your available resources. Take an inventory beforehand to avoid finding copy paper at 3 AM.

Your main resources are time and money. Whenever possible, spend money instead of time. You can make/get/steal more money. You can save time and use your time efficiently, but you can't make more of the stuff this side of Stephen Hawking.

Getting the work out quickly means you'll be able to handle more projects; it means happier clients, it means you can bill sooner and have that much more cash on hand.

Technology

One way to spend money to save or "make time" is through technology. Technology is a wonderful thing (OK, when it works). Always available, never takes a vacation, endlessly flexible, and no one will ever knock on your door asking about payroll taxes and workman's comp.

There are many job-specific apps, software packages, and third-party platforms (with more coming every day) that you can access on an as-needed basis to make your work life more efficient and your life-life easier. Many offer a free seven to thirty-day trial, after which there will be a small monthly fee, but you can cancel your subscription as soon as it's no longer useful.

Suggested Project Management Software

1. monday.com is a Work Operating System (Work OS) designed to help teams work without limits when it comes to project and task management. Monday work management offers a user-friendly and intuitive interface with a range of customizable features that cater to the specific collaboration and communication needs of any team across industries.

2. Trello is a web-based project management tool that uses a board-based approach to help individuals and teams organize their tasks and projects. It is a popular and user- friendly tool that allows users to easily track their progress, collaborate with team members, and visualize their workflow simply and intuitively.

3. Basecamp is a project management tool that helps teams to stay organized, collaborate efficiently, and complete projects on time. It was first launched in 2004 by 37Signals, but later rebranded as Basecamp in 2014. Basecamp is a cloud-based project management software that can be accessed through a web browser, desktop, or mobile application.

4. Wrike is a cloud-based project management software designed to help teams streamline their workflows and collaborate more effectively. It was founded in 2006 by Andrew Filev and has since grown into a popular tool used by businesses of all sizes to manage projects from start to finish.

5. Asana is a popular project management tool designed to help teams collaborate and manage their tasks and projects more efficiently. Asana has gained a reputation as a reliable and easy-to-use tool for project management, and it is used by many businesses and organizations around the world.

Do a search for what you need to do (video conversion, for instance), and you'll be surprised at what you find.

Move the Project off of our Desk onto to Someone Else's

Regardless of the size of your business, you'll need to build a team. In the heat of battle, you might think that it's faster to do something yourself than to take the time to explain what you want to a temp. WROOOOOOOOOONG! Having just one extra pair of hands frees you up to prepare for the next phase or take regular bathroom breaks.

Take care to hire the right people. I always start new freelancers off with some small, low-priority, and, frankly, boring assignment. It's a test. If they can take such a project seriously, I know I can trust them with something more important.

A word of caution: increasingly, people are finding most freelancers via the web or email introductions. Face-to-face introductions are becoming a rarity. Consider the big picture. If your new hire lives in a remote corner of the woods and is always available anytime, day or night, you may have found a budding Unabomber.

After trying several long-distance options, I have found that face-to-face contact is still the best way to give directions and clear up any miscommunications. Emailing, texting, Skyping, and Facetiming, are all fine as far as they go, but nothing beats showing up on someone's doorstep and asking them, "What the hell is going on." ZOOM is another good option.

Give the Client "Homework"

My favorite technique. Collaborate with your clients, and make them part of the process. It makes them feel involved and keeps miscommunications to a minimum. I find it especially useful to keep them busy while I'm on vacation.

Some clients may complain that you are asking them to do the job they are paying you. That's not really the case. They understand their business better than you do, and they are a valuable source of information, and since they are paying you for your time, anything they can do to save you time will ultimately save them money. They may not buy that last argument, but it's worth a try.

The larger issue here is that many clients use smaller or entrepreneurial companies as a cost-saving measure. There must be some acknowledgment that such firms can charge less because they have fewer employees (and overhead) than larger ones.

They simply cannot expect the same level of service. If they want you to work with them on the fees, they may have to work with you on timing.

The Power of Stalling

I'm not talking about bailing out on a job so you can go hang out at Denny's. If it allows you to do a better job, selectively stalling is not bad. You may need an extra day or two to sharpen the presentation, define the parameters, or get things in order.

There will also come a time when you'll have conflicting demands on your resources, and working 96 hours straight really isn't an option. Many times you can resolve the situation with a simple phone call. Most clients are fairly reasonable and will accommodate you the best they can.

For the others? Ignoring phone messages and emails is bad business, but sometimes...

Remember, effective project management requires a combination of technical skills, leadership abilities, and effective communication. Continuously refine your project management approach based on your experiences and feedback from your team members and clients.

QUIZ

Choose the Correct Course of Action:

True or False:

_____ The goal of project management is to move the project from your desk to somebody else's desk.

_____ When in doubt, resign and leave the problem for the next guy.

_____ Giving the client homework fosters collaboration.

_____ Breaking your work into manageable steps only causes delays.

_____ Allocating resources is one of the main functions of project management.

_____ Hiding in the bathroom when things go wrong forces people to figure things out themselves.

_____ The term "Project Creep" refers to an uncooperative client.

_____ Developing an internal process ensures things will get done efficiently.

_____ When all else fails, weep.

Chapter 9:

Client
Management

Keeping them happy...
within reason

WARNING: The following chapter contains material that may not be suitable for novice entrepreneurs. Do not attempt these techniques yourself without first consulting a professional.

It's been said of advertising that it would be a pretty good business if it weren't for the clients. Clients come in all shapes, sizes, and temperaments. They can be the source of all things good, and, in some cases, they can literally be a necessary evil.

But take heart! You need not be at their mercy.

THEY called YOU, remember? And though some of them would rather not admit it, you have, or can do, something they really need.

Jumping through hoops—NOT.

Many entrepreneurs make the mistake of approaching client relations from a subservient point of view. Phrases such as "The customer is always right," "Make each of your clients feel like they're your only one," and "When they say jump, I ask how high" illustrate the lengths to which some business owners will go to retain their clients/customers.

Unless you have a pathological desire to be "needed," these platitudes are useless. Of course, you have multiple clients, each with conflicting personalities and needs. They all can't "be right" or "be the most important." And I never really understood the whole "jumping" thing.

 (Whenever a client has asked me to jump, I've always said, "Let's think about this for a minute. Are you sure you need me to jump? Might you be better off if I skipped, or hopped, or turned cartwheels? For some reason, this sort of question never comes up again.)

Most importantly, you have your own business to run and what's good for the client isn't always good for you. What if Client A insists that you spend the day at their place, Client B is very sorry, but they need another round of last-minute revisions, Client C demands a justification for the last seven invoices, while Client D is in need of a nap and is very, very cranky. How do you handle this unruly pack of competing demands on your time and resources, short of crawling off into a corner with a pint of Wild Turkey or Chocolate Häagen Dazs, or on bad days, both?

In formulating my methodology, I have been influenced by the findings of a behavioral specialist who has done extensive work in this area, one who truly understands the inner psychology of leadership, group dynamics, and butt-sniffing.

I am, of course, referring to Cesar Milan, The Dog Whisperer. In a nutshell, Mr. Milan's approach combines exercise, discipline, and reward with a sensitivity to the subject's mental state or "energy." (You can find clips of Cesar in action on YouTube).

At the core of Mr. Milan's philosophy is the concept of "Being a Pack Leader." Dogs are simple creatures with basic needs. They are looking for a Pack Leader to set boundaries, establish order, and lead them to the proper course of action.

Likewise, clients hire you because they have a basic need that is outside their area of expertise. They are looking for someone to set boundaries, establish order, and lead them to the proper course of action. I am suggesting you become "The Client Whisperer."

According to Mr. Milan, Pack Leader is calm and assertive. Pack Leader does not explain. Pack Leader does not ask permission— and I might add, Pack Leader doesn't engage in random jumping.

By now, many of you think this is suitable for Shih Tzus or Labradoodles, but in my experience, clients are more like ill-behaved Rottweilers.

Exactly how does this thing work? Let me offer an example:

I had a client who was a real "Pitbull." Short, a little pudgy, with thinning hair—he obviously had a difficult adolescence and was taking it out on the rest of the world. Maybe all he needed was a hug, but he wasn't paying me for hugs. Hugs are extra.

Every week we held a marketing meeting where the team would gather around the conference table and present him with the past week's efforts. Each report would be greeted with various questions, challenges, expletives, and the occasional off-topic rant. It would go something like this:

Alan: "So, Greg, where are we with the renovations on the second floor?"

Greg, the Project Manager: "The sheetrock came in on Thursday, and we're on schedule to finish up this week."

Alan: "On schedule? What kind of a friggin' project manager are you? A monkey can bring things in on schedule. I'm not paying you to be on schedule.' Get off your ass and tell those clowns who work for you to stop screwing around and get this done AHEAD of schedule. The longer this takes, the more it's costing me. Nobody wants to work anymore! The other day I walked into Best Buy. I'm looking around for a new flat screen, and the next thing I know, I'm surrounded by refrigerators. I'm standing there like a jerk waiting for someone to help me."

You get the picture

Usually, I just said my piece and tried to ignore the rest, but one day, just before it was my turn, I found myself thinking, "Pack Leader does not explain, Pack Leader does not ask permission." I looked him in the eye, paused momentarily, and calmly began.

Me: "Alan, here are the brochure revisions we talked about last week. The new copy is in place, I reworked the third panel and moved the photos around as discussed. I did not change the photo on the cover because it now works better with the new copy."

"Oh," Alan exclaimed. He seemed a bit disoriented, as though things had happened differently than expected, and he was now out of sync.

Alan: "So, ah, Pilla, what about all that environmental stuff," Alan's company was applying for some"Green Certification," so he wanted to ensure that his printed material was as environmentally friendly as possible.

Me: "Alan," I said, using the same tone of voice one would use to get the attention of a Doberman, "we are printing this on recycled paper and using soy-based inks."

Alan: "That any good?'" he asked.

Me: "By the time I'm finished, you'll be able to eat this brochure."

He replied by saying, "Oh," again with that same puzzled look and moved on to torment the sales director.

I was "calm and assertive," which triggered a "passive-submissive" response. Maybe it was a coincidence, and maybe it worked because Alan IS part Pitbull, but the point is, I remained calm and focused and "claimed my turf" or, in this case, my piece of the conference table.

Be the Pack Leader

Start by being a Pack Leader

Being a Pack Leader is a matter of attitude, of remaining Calm and Assertive at all times. It means leading your clients to the best possible outcome, seeing that they get what they need rather than just giving them what they want.

If you had a medical problem and had to have surgery, would you let the Doctor do his job or would you draw a dotted line on your body and write the words "Cut Here"? Would you really want to go to a Surgeon who only did what you told them? Would you deal with someone who drew diagrams on their body? Creepy.

Regardless of your business or profession, your customers/clients came to you for your knowledge and experience. You owe them the benefit of that expertise, even if they protest.

Understand their needs: Take the time to thoroughly understand your client's requirements, goals, and expectations. Actively listen to their concerns and ask clarifying questions to ensure you have a clear understanding of their needs.

Establish clear communication channels: Determine the preferred communication methods and frequency with your clients. This could include regular meetings, email updates, or a project management software platform. Ensure that communication is timely, transparent, and consistent.

Set realistic expectations: Be honest and transparent about what can be achieved within the given constraints. Clearly define project timelines, deliverables, and potential limitations. Manage expectations by providing regular updates on progress, challenges, and changes.

Provide regular progress updates: Keep your clients informed about the project's status, accomplishments, and any potential issues. Regularly communicate milestones, completed tasks, and upcoming activities. Sharing progress reports or visual representations of progress can be helpful.

Be proactive in problem-solving: Anticipate potential issues or challenges and be proactive in addressing them. If you encounter obstacles or delays, communicate them to your clients promptly and offer potential solutions or alternative approaches.

Manage changes effectively: Changes are inevitable in most projects. Establish a clear change management process that outlines how changes will be assessed, communicated, and implemented. Discuss the impact of changes on timelines, budgets, and resources with your clients and gain their agreement before proceeding.

Document agreements and changes: Keep a record of all agreements, decisions, and changes made during the project. This helps avoid misunderstandings and provides a reference point in case of disputes or conflicts.

Conduct post-project reviews: Once the project is completed, conduct a post-project review with your clients to gather feedback. Assess their satisfaction, identify areas for improvement, and capture lessons learned for future projects.

Be Objective: Speak with confidence and frame all of your advice in terms that objectively addresses their problems and concerns. Avoid subjective terms like "I think," "I like," or "It seems to me . . ." If it comes down to a matter of opinion, the client will figure that since they are paying the bill, they'll follow their gut instead of yours.

Focus on the Work

To quote Michael Corleone in The Godfather, Part I, "See, Tom, it's business, not personal." Personality differences, questionable behavior, bad hair — everybody has something. You were hired to do a job and, insofar as those little quirks don't interfere, ignore them and stay focused on what you do best.

Don't Suck Up

Keep the relationship on an equal footing and avoid the urge to become a "Yes Man," "Yes Woman," or, if you prefer, "A Person of Yes." While this might gain you some temporary advantage, you risk losing credibility, and you could start doubting yourself, which will lead to the client doubting you. Remember, they hired you because you are the expert. If you let yourself get pressured into some bad decisions, guess who gets the big finger pointed at them when things fall apart?

Need-to-Know Basis

Only tell them what they need to know, and keep extraneous information to a minimum. They really don't need to know about your personal life, office gossip, or the fact that the hard drive containing all their files crashed and was hacked into yesterday, but it's all OK now.

Be Polite, but Be Strong

Al Capone reportedly said, "You can get a lot further with a smile and a gun than you can with just a smile." While I am not advocating using firearms in your business dealings, I will note that even someone as ruthless as "Scarface" realized the importance of maintaining a pleasant demeanor.

Always Deliver

The best marketing plan for an entrepreneur is to do a really good job. For the vast number of clients, the respect they'll have for you is based on how well you perform, and all those project-related problems can magically disappear if they are happy with the results.

Getting Primal: Food and Booze

Clients are people too, and, if appropriate, it's good to get them away from the workplace so you can relate on a human level. I've handled many difficult situations by meeting with clients in a bar or restaurant and hashing things out person to person. Buy them lunch, take them out for drinks, show them a good time, but not too good a time—you might even become friends. If the words "incriminating photos" work their way into a later conversation, you may have overdone it.

Personality Conflicts

Despite your best efforts, personality conflicts may start to overwhelm the project. Certain people rub each other the wrong way, often unintentionally. If you're really not getting along, but you still need to work with this person, you may need a buffer — something, or someone, that will allow you to communicate without direct contact.

Be creative with email, text messages, voice mail, Facebook, Twitter, and cyber- people. There is almost no end to how you can communicate with someone not-so-close and impersonal.

See Them in Person

On the other hand, nothing drives home the fact that you're a force to be reckoned with more than showing up (by appointment) in their office and confirming your presence in the physical world. Ignoring that overdue invoice is hard when you're sitting in their office. Refusing to leave is optional.

Also, seeing them in their natural element can give you a better idea of whom you're dealing with. I had a client who was very condescending because, at the time, I was a "one-man band." He kept dropping hints that my business was too small and unprofessional. When I finally visited his office, it turned out he was working out of a tiny space sandwiched between a tattoo parlor and an auto parts store.

As a Last Resort

If the relationship does end, remain professional. There's even a chance that they'll realize the error of their ways and want you back. Don't get mad, pad the bill! A strategically placed one or zero can greatly restore your sense of well-being.

Remember, effective client management is about building trust, maintaining clear communication, and delivering value. By focusing on their needs and fostering a positive working relationship, you can enhance client satisfaction and create long-term partnerships.

QUIZ
Choose the Correct Course of Action:

What does a Pack Leader never do?
A. Prepare boxed lunches
B. Advise on how to properly fill a suitcase
C. Explain or ask permission
D. Turn his back on his pack

How should you approach a "Pit Bull" client?
A. From behind
B. In a calm but assertive manner
C. By email
D. As little as possible

Which of these should you NOT DO?
A. Focus on the work
B. Stay objective
C. Take everything personally, show your pouty lip whenever possible
D Always deliver on your promises

What is the basic goal of Client Management?
A. Get in, get paid, get out
B. Guide the client to a mutually satisfactory solution
C. Bend the client to your will
D. Make friends for life

Chapter 10:

Getting Help

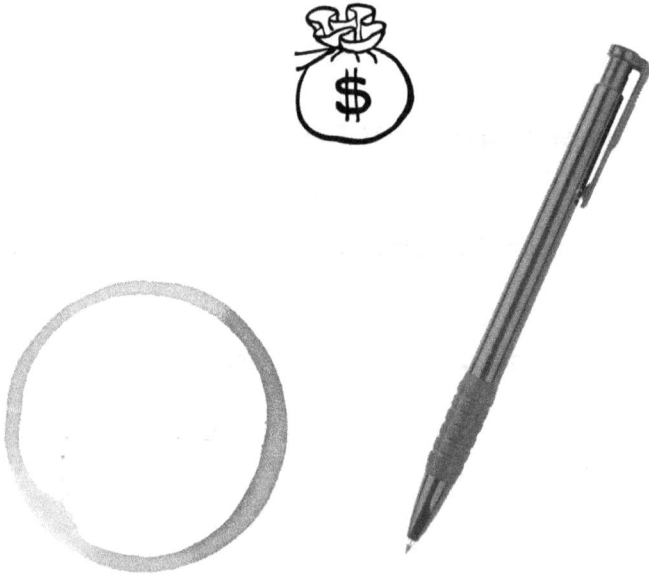

Working for yourself does not mean working by yourself

Many entrepreneurs start out as "solopreneurs," the stereotypical workaholic who conducts business from their home, keeps ridiculous hours and puts off housekeeping and regular sleep. But even the most self-sufficient and/or anti-social among us will eventually need help.

This is especially true since the key to entrepreneurial success is to spend less time working "in" your business and more time working "on" your business. You may have started your company because you love what you do, but in order to grow, you have to do less of it, and more of things like business development, client relations, and yes, even bookkeeping.

In other words, there is only so much you can do by yourself, and since running your own business requires that you wear many hats, it's a good idea to have more than one head to put them on.

Chat GPT

Artificial intelligence is the latest and most controversial addition to the "workforce." At this writing, ChatGPT was the first to be widely used by the business community. It is a natural language processing tool driven by AI technology, allowing you to have human-like conversations. The language model can answer questions and assist you with tasks like writing the first draft of articles, reports, essays, presentations, composing emails, and even coding.

I use it for research, and it can give me in seconds what it might have taken me hours or days to find on Google. " There have been serious questions about its accuracy, so as Ronald Reagan often said to Gorbachov, "Trust, but verify.

There are concerns about workers and students submitting work they did not actually lay their hands on, in addition to worries among designers and visual artists about plagiarism. Since AI aggregates existing material, any artwork it creates is derivative and, by definition, violates somebody's copyright.

With those caveats in mind, here are some of the ways AI can assist small businesses:

Customer support: AI-powered chatbots can handle customer inquiries and provide basic support 24/7. They can respond to common questions, guide customers through the purchasing process, and even escalate complex issues to human representatives when necessary.

Personalization: AI algorithms can analyze customer data and behavior to provide personalized recommendations, offers, and content. This level of personalization helps businesses tailor their marketing efforts to individual customers, improving customer satisfaction and boosting sales.

Data analysis: AI algorithms can process and analyze large amounts of data quickly and efficiently. Small businesses can leverage AI to gain insights from customer data, market trends, and internal operations. This information can be used to make data-driven decisions, optimize operations, and identify growth opportunities.

Automation: AI can automate repetitive and time-consuming tasks, freeing up valuable time for small business owners and employees. Tasks such as data entry, inventory management, and social media posting can be automated, allowing staff to focus on more strategic and value-added activities.

Lead generation: Chat GPT can engage with potential customers and collect information to generate leads. By interacting with website visitors or through messaging platforms, Chat GPT can ask qualifying questions, provide product information, and capture contact details. The sales team can use this data to follow up with leads and convert them into customers.

Sales assistance: Chat GPT can act as a virtual sales assistant by guiding customers through the sales process. It can provide information about product features, compare different options, and offer additional incentives or discounts to encourage purchases. Chat GPT can also handle objections and provide relevant information to address customer concerns.

Upselling and cross-selling: Chat GPT can identify opportunities for upselling or cross-selling by understanding customer needs and preferences. It can suggest complementary products or services, highlight bundle offers, or recommend upgrades to increase the average order value and maximize sales revenue.

Competitive analysis: AI-powered tools can gather and analyze data about competitors, market trends, and consumer preferences. This information can help small businesses identify gaps in the market, track competitor strategies, and adjust their own offerings accordingly.

See the Resourse Section at the end of the book more information.

Carefully consider your specific needs, budget, and the level of expertise. Working with AI experts or leveraging user-friendly AI platforms can make it easier for small businesses to adopt and benefit from AI technologies.

sPeope who need people

There are many levels of help out there, from the basic office support you can get from Kinko's or Staples to using individual freelancers such as yourself to actually hiring a live human being and having them appear in your office, to Artificial Intelligence

Before we start, however, I'd like to share a few ground rules I've developed over the years to ensure that the help is actually "helping."

Working with Freelancers: Where Do You Find These People?

So you've decided to give in and get yourself some assistance. What now? You have several options:

The first and best place to go is to other professionals such as yourself. Ask around; get some referrals. Chances are that people who have delivered for others will deliver for you, and this way, you are starting off with some personal connection.

Your next option is —surprise— the internet. Post a request on LinkedIn, Craigslist, Facebook, and Twitter. (If you don't already belong to one of those sites, I must ask, "Why?") There are many sites that put businesses with work together with people looking for work.

Platforms that supply you with freelance help

1. Fiverr —Fiverr is an online marketplace that connects freelancers offering digital services in 500+ categories.to people or businesses looking to hire. See fiverr.com

2. Toptal— An exclusive network of the top freelance software developers, designers, finance experts, product managers, and project managers in the world. See toptal.com

3. Freelancer.com—The world's largest freelance marketplace. See freelancer.com

4. Upwork—The largest network of independent professionals and get things done—from quick turnarounds to big transformations. See upwork.com

5. Guru—Create your free job posting and start receiving Quotes within hours. Find and hire expert freelancers. Compare the Quotes you receive and hire the best freelance professionals. See guru.com

Off-Site Freelancers

First stop, other shut-ins such as yourself. Unless you have development money or bankruptcy is part of your master plan, it's a good idea not to hire staff immediately. Plenty of freelancers, just like you, will be only too glad to lend a hand for a fee.

In this cyber age, help is often an email away. I have working relationships with people I've never seen. It's a bit eerie, like communication with someone on another planet. You send your work out into the cybersphere and wait for it to be returned safely to the Earth.

What I wrote before about clear requirements goes double here. Email/phone communication leaves too much to the imagination, miscommunications should almost be assumed. It once took me months to straighten out an e-commerce site because the client and the three different programmers I ended up having to hire all had a different understanding of the words "Checkout," "Shopping Cart," "Payment Gateway," and apparently, "Deadline."

The Amazing Disappearing Freelancers are people who work remotely from remote locations and have fewer social skills than the Unabomber. They can be a bit prickly and can disappear at any moment—anything can happen to them. You may be waiting days for a project to be completed, happily unaware that a bear has eaten your programmer.

Delegate With a Purpose

Don't just throw work at people and hope for the best. Have a clear idea of what you want help with, then define the task as specifically as possible. Give clear directions, and make sure the directions are understood. Many entrepreneurs fall into the trap of thinking that it will take longer to explain something than it will to do it themselves.

This is a delusion, possibly caused by the fear of losing control or the fallout from inept toilet training. If done correctly, thirty minutes spent making yourself clear can free you up for days—I know, I've timed it.

Show Them, and Yourself, the Money

Agree on costs and terms at the beginning. How much will it cost? When is it due? What are the terms? There is nothing worse than having a project held up at the last minute because of a dispute over the fee.

I once—and only once—used a freelancer who would not turn over a completed project because he had "a policy" of getting paid on delivery. Of course, he did not inform me of said policy beforehand. Suddenly I felt like a hostage negotiator trying to "free" my work. I eventually had to leave a check in a plain white envelope with someone named "Lenny" in exchange for a CD.

Look to Form Relationships

Bring people in with an eye toward building a team, so you are not starting from scratch with every project. The more you work with the same people, the better you will understand each other, and the less they will feel like just cogs in your machine.

Project Management

Remember that when you hire someone, you are vouching for their performance. You are now responsible for other people's work, for keeping things on schedule and budget, and for quality control. If things go wrong, you're the one getting yelled at. (See the earlier chapter about Project Management for more information and Tips and Tricks.)

When it's Over, it's Over.

If it's not working out, complete the assignment, thank them profusely, and never speak to them again. Now that we've gotten that straight — let's get you some help.

Basic Office Support

Where once we had copy shops and office supply stores, we now have "Business Centers." Besides paper clips, you can also get everything from copies to printing to tech support. I suppose they don't have an espresso bar because then there'd be no reason to leave. Depending on how close you are to one, these places are very convenient for copies, simple flyers, faxing (remember faxing?), and so on.

Some places will take orders via email, so you don't even have to leave your place of business. But beware, the quality can be spotty. The people running your job probably worked in the stockroom a few days ago. Many times, I've seen them run to the instruction manual to answer why a print job that didn't quite meet the vision of its creator. It's best you have realistic expectations—keep it simple, and allow for delays and do- overs. Remember, your rush project may be what's keeping someone from going to lunch.

Vendors

These are other companies you buy stuff from. Though technically not staff, a good vendor can save you time and money and make you look great. Depending on the nature of your business, these are other professionals and small businesses such as photographers, IT specialists, certified inspectors, and, in extreme cases, private detectives. Be sure to comparison-shop and be a good customer. Make them feel like they are a part of your team. The principle of "what goes- around-comes-around" is very much in play here, especially if you find yourself needing a favor. Also, other businesses are a great source of referrals. You give business to them; there's no reason why they can't give business to you.

When Things Get Busy, Interns

Most schools have intern programs that allow students to work for credits and real-world experience (translation "For Free"). The results can be uneven. Most of them are eager, perky young things with more enthusiasm than experience, but that's why they're students! If you have realistic expectations and clearly define their duties, they can be very helpful. If you're lucky, you may be looking at future employees.

On-Site Freelancers/Employees

If you have the space, having a live, warm human being working in your office is the way to go. Miscommunication is minimal. You can keep track of their work, they are available for emergencies, and as your comfort level goes up, you can delegate more responsibilities to them and spend more of your time growing the biz instead of doing the work.

Stick to freelance at first, but beware of the Labor Department. Many companies, particularly Ad Agencies, have tried to skirt labor laws by hiring "full-time" freelancers rather than full-fledged employees. Also, once you hire someone, you face all sorts of hurdles in getting rid of them. Every employee brings with them a potential harassment suit, and every day brings another form of discrimination you can be sued for. "I'm a tea drinker, and you only have a coffee machine. You are practicing "beverage-ism" and forcing me to go to the corner Deli."

Know who you are hiring

Then there's the question of how well do you know these people anyway. They may be their best during the interview process and not let their "Freak Flag" fly until AFTER you hire them. Soon you're dealing with outrageous clothing, annoying personal habits, and previously unseen tattoos—I had a guy tell me, halfway through a project, that he was a warlock.

Then there's always the possibility that the perfectly reasonable assistant you just took on will turn into a raving, potentially dangerous lunatic once you tell them, "I don't think this is working out. I'll have to let you go." I know someone who had to call the cops and hide out in the bathroom until the police arrived.

When it's time to go, go carefilly

If you find yourself in this situation, do not personalize the situation. If you are dealing with frelancers you can simply pay them what you owe them, and never call them again. With an actual full time employee you may have to work around the labor laws.

Even though you have the right to fire anybody at anytime, charges of like racism, sexism, or ageism may be thrown at you by someone who simpley refuses to leave. Document their performance, or lack thereof, so you can show a pattern of bad work habits in case you get hauled into an arbitration.

Other Professionals, Partners, Associates, Collaborators

Once you have a handle on your core business, think about teaming up with other businesses/professionals, expanding your capabilities, and moving into other areas. You can share resources, expertise, contacts, and so on. The best of these relationships can be extremely synergistic, and they don't have to be any more formal than a handshake. A caterer may want to hook up with an Event Planner, a designer with a copywriter, a Real Estate Broker with a Title Agent— tradesman, such as Carpenters, Plumbers, and Electricians, regularly team up.

Howdy, Partner

If things go really well, you might even consider a full-blown partnership, though you may not want to tinker with a good thing. Taking your business in another direction or breaking up with an associate is easy with an informal relationship. Once you've formalized your partnership, you may not have the freedom you once had, and any change requires negotiations, paperwork, and legal fees.

Be careful that these "partners" don't steal your clients. Make sure the parameters of the relationship are clearly defined. Trust needs to be earned. I've mistakenly given a "partner" total access to one of my clients. They got so close that I have good reason to believe they had an affair. When I met one of her clients, I was read the riot act for handing out a business card.

Family Members

And finally, we come to a resource that's close to home. It may even be IN your home: members of your family. Having a well-connected family member can be a real asset.

Many a successful business has been started by a strategically placed phone call, investment, or job offer made by somebody's uncle, cousin, or parent.

On the other hand, hiring family members can be tricky. Depending on the amount of baggage a particular relationship has, every request is fraught with emotional peril. For example, asking an idle second cousin to help out with the clerical work could result in something like, "Why are you asking me to make copies? Is it because you think I have no imagination? You never supported my dream to become the tallest ballerina in Essex County. I hate you." Tread carefully.

Children fall into two categories:

Small children are all too eager to help, but depending on age and attention span, and reading level, there may not be all that much they can do to help out. "Here ya go, honey, sit on this stack of papers and make sure they don't blow away." may be the best they can do.

College-age children may actually have some skills, and if they are interested in following in your footsteps, they may see this as a great learning opportunity. But if that's not the case, be grateful for any help you can get: filing, running errands, answering the phone, keeping erstwhile prima ballerinas at bay.

Pets

I have an eight-pound black toy poodle named Decker who basically functions as the office "Concierge." When I'm engrossed in a project or on the phone, I don't always hear when there's someone at the door. Nothing gets by Decker, however, who will let me know if anyone is approaching within a half-block.

He once spent a day and a half barking at a corner of my office for no apparent reason. The next day my cable/internet connection went out. It turns out a squirrel had chewed through the wiring in the same corner Decker had been barking at. Had I only listened.

He also lets me know when the mail is here, when it's time for lunch, and when it's time to "go outside."

QUIZ

Choose the Correct
Course of Action:

Match the personnel to the task:

A. **Freelance Help**
B. **Off-site help**
C. **Professional Associates**
D. **Partners**
E. **Family Members**
F. **Pets**

_____ A team of unknown programmers in an undisclosed Southeast Asian country.

_____ Call Uncle Fred and thank him for the intro to "the guy."

_____ Alerts you when the mail has arrived, shares your lunch, and lets you know when it's time to go "outside."

_____ Accompanies you to a pitch meeting, adding their capabilities to yours to create an "uber company."

_____ A trusted friend in the same business who can commiserate with you over drinks.

_____ A member of your virtual team whom you work with on a project basis, even though you've never met in person.

Chapter 11:

Branding

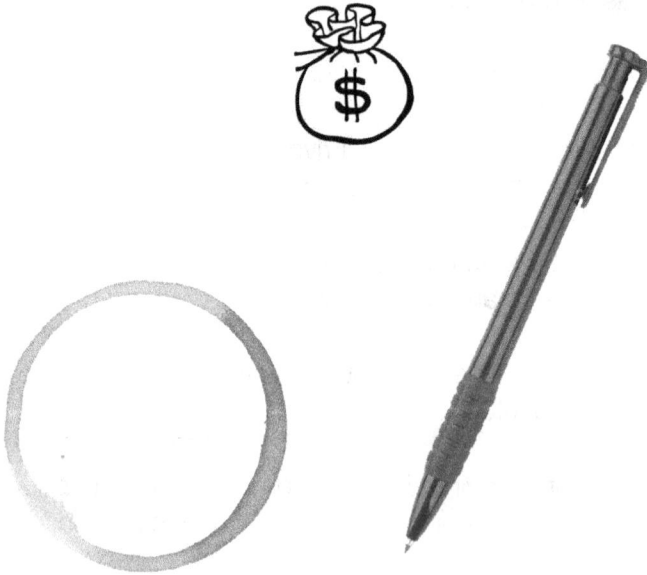

ME Inc.
A WHOLLY OWNED SUBSIDARY OF YOU

Just who do you think you are?

No areas of entrepreneurship is as misunderstood and under-appreciated as branding and marketing. Some ignore it completely, some try to do it themselves, and some see it as an opportunity to help out the less fortunate. In the past, discerning business people who agonize over every minute detail will gleefully put their company's identity campaign and advertising into the hands of an unemployed buddy or inexperienced family member.

Thanks to social media, now businesses of all sizes, and even indiviuals, spend a considerable amout of time and resources establishing a public identity.

You need many things to set up a new business. You need a lawyer, an accountant, a business coach, and an assistant. You need to purchase equipment, furniture, and some manner of office space. But of all the things needed to set up your business, marketing is the only activity whose sole purpose is to generate income.

In a world dominated by mass marketing, branding was the concern of large multinational corporations. It required large budgets, legions of writers, designers, marketing analysts, brand managers, lawyers, and so on. They poured countless hours and countless dollars into determining, defining, and defending the Corporate Identity.

But Branding is just as important for Small Businesses that face increased local competition and need to make every marketing dollar count. A memorable local identity leads to "word-of-mouth" referrals and offsets the fact that you don't have the bucks to be constantly badgering your target audience with a massive ad campaign.

The Small Business Advantage

I've heard many small business owners say that they can't afford or do not need a branding campaign. They see themselves as straightforward, down-to-earth people who don't need fancy bells and whistles to attract new business. Most of their clients come through word of mouth. Their work speaks for itself. But even if your work speaks for itself, everybody can't hear it, and you never know about the work you're not getting.

Promoting yourself is a crucial part of running your own show.

Small Businesses have an advantage over their multi-national competitors. Small Businesses deal directly with their customers daily—talking to them, servicing them, and hearing them complain. It's a never-ending exercise in consumer research.

Small Businesses are in a position to create emotional connections with their target audience, something corporate behemoths can only dream of—if they could dream.

Before You Start: Hire a Professional

Avoid the temptation to do this yourself. First, it will look like you did it yourself. Second, you have enough to do (see the rest of this book).

You use the appropriate professionals for other aspects of your business, so why not here? A marketing professional brings experience and a needed measure of objectivity—looking at your business from the viewpoint of a potential customer. And since this is all they do, it will actually get done.

Avoid the temptation to go with the lowest bid. This is not the place to be stingy. Instead of saving money, you could wind up wasting it on work that is unusable. Invest in yourself, and pay to get things right.

Who Do You Think You Are, and Why Should Anybody Care?

"Branding" is a term that gets thrown around a lot these days. To some, it's a carefully crafted statement of who you are as a company that permeates everything from your identity to your marketing material to how you handle customer service. To others, it's putting a logo on a pencil. To most, it's somewhere in between.

Basically, Branding is about defining your business. In order to do that successfully, I have found it useful to start by asking the following questions:

- Why do you do what you do? Define the reason you are in business.
- What is the nature of your business? Define your specific product or service.
- Who are you doing it for? Define your target market.
- How do you do it better than the next guy? Define the way you do what you do

If you do find yourself mired in the business equivalent of an "identity crisis," there are a number of approaches you can try.

Branding Option #1 Finding Your Brand Personality

Some marketing consultants use a "Brand Personality Quiz," much like an IQ test or those compatibility tests one often finds in the back of women's magazines. The consultant presents you with seemingly irrelevant questions designed to get you thinking "outside of the box" and reveal your true entrepreneurial self. They then take these answers, tally up your score, and send you a report and bill.

The questions usually look something like this:

• If your business were a tree, what kind of tree would it be?

• If your business were throwing a party, what kind of food would it serve?

• A Priest, a Rabbi, and your business are sitting in a rowboat. Who mans the tiller?

•Your business walks into a Doctor's office and says, "Doc, it hurts when I do this." What color are the Doctor's suspenders? (This is a trick question. You can't see the suspenders under the lab coat.)

Branding Option #2
The Unique Sales Proposition (USP)

This is the traditional approach used by most brands. The idea is to focus on the unique quality of your product or service, the one thing you have that no one else has, and the primary benefit it bestows upon the consumer. The problem here is that most companies are not all that unique, so they make something up.

In the 1960s, a household cleanser's USP was that it was the only one with "Chlorinol," a chemical compound that only existed in the imagination of their ad agency. Predictably, it was later claimed to be "New and Improved" because it now contained "Super Chlorinol." One can only assume that Super Duper Ultra Chlorinol was in development.

Branding Option #4 Finding Your "Why"
The Most Effective Way to Define Your Brand

"People will buy why you do something before they buy what you do."
—*TED Talker Simon Sinek*

Finding and communicating your passion sets you apart from your competitors and inspires like-minded, incredibly loyal customers. Iconic brands become iconic because they stand for more than just widgets. They sell an idea. Yes, they deliver on their promises, but they also touch something deeper in their customers, creating a feeling of belonging.

The best example of this is Apple Computer. Their "Why" is "Empowering and uplifting people through technology." They do this by offering products that are inventive, beautiful to look at, and easy to use. They "just happen" to sell computers. Notice all of their advertising features what people can do with their technology, not the technology itself.

You'll never see the word "megahertz" in an Apple ad. Visit any Apple Store, anytime, not just during a new product introduction, and you'll see what customer loyalty looks like.

Defining or redefining your "Why" can sometimes transform your business and even your industry.

Faced with competition from the industrial ice cream makers, the makers of what is now Häagen Dazs realized that they could not compete on price, so they decided to compete on quality. They redefined their "Why" to providing a high-quality product for people with discriminating tastes and created the Premium Ice Cream category. Snob appeal paid off in the form of loyal customers who are willing to pay more for a better product with social cache. Starbucks would later do something similar with coffee.

In reality, the name "Häagen Dazs" is totally fictitious. Based in the Bronx, NY, they created the illusion of being Scandinavian—and went so far as to print a map of Norway on the lid of their ice cream containers even though the closest they ever got to Oslo was an occasional can of sardines. As a fellow Bronxite, it makes me proud.

Branding Options #2 Archetype Branding

A more psychological approach is to tap into the marketplace's collective consciousness and build a brand around one of the "Psychological Archetypes" identified by Swiss psychologist and Freud groupie Carl Jung. (An archetype can best be described as either a pattern of behavior that all people recognize subconsciously or the results of a personality test one often finds in the back of women's magazines). Some of the better-known Archetypes and their corporate manifestations are as follows:

The Hero: "Stand Aside, Puny Human . . ."

Heroes love a challenge and are able to leap tall problems in a single brainstorming session. They are focused, confident, capable, results-oriented, and good at inspiring others. They are better than you are.

Examples: Microsoft, Amazon, Nike, FedEx, the U.S Army

The Caregiver: "Just Sit There, I'll Get That for You . . ."

Like a favorite aunt who never forgets a birthday, Caregivers tend to everyone's needs. They create a warm, caring environment and stable, nurturing relationships. They'll always be there for you—even though you never call.

Examples: Campbell's Soup, Allstate Insurance

The Rebel: "Rules!? We Dun't Need No Stinkin' Rules . . ."

They zig when everyone else zags. It appears they're only happy when they're making trouble, but Rebel organizations are successful at developing radical ideas, products, and services if only to spite everyone who said it couldn't be done.

Examples: Apple, Harley Davidson, Virgin Anything

A variation of this approach utilizes "The Sinatra Scale," based on Frank Sinatra's iconic hit "That's Life," where a brand profile is determined to be that of a Puppet, a Pauper, a Pirate, a Poet, a Pawn or a King.

Basic Branding Materials:

Glad you figured yourself out—now what?

Once you have arrived at your identity, you're ready to move on to marketing your business. We'll get into that in the next chapter, but you'll need a few items to make it "real."

Written Guidelines

Your branding decisions create a foundation for all the marketing material to come, giving your company a consistent, readily recognized identity that will appeal to your target audience. You'll probably have a number of website designers, social media experts, freelancers, interns, printers, and producers of stuff creating things for your business. Written Branding Guidelines that give specifications for fonts, colors, messaging, photos, videos, and so on will ensure that it all looks like it comes from you and not some crazed group of people whom all have the same name and address.

The Logo

The cornerstone of your identity is your logo. You'll need some identifiable symbol, trademark, or type treatment that accurately reflects and readily identifies your business in the marketplace. There are countless approaches available. Whichever one you choose, your logo should be something you're comfortable with, something you can show to current and potential clients without cringing.

Resist the urge to use websites that turn creating your logo into a contest. For $99 or $65, or even $5, you'll get unlimited submissions. Since anyone can make a submission, the talent level ranges from desperate professionals with too much downtime to high school students who think this would be fun. Your logo is too important to be trusted to an anonymous, random individual. Hire a pro who will meet with you, take the time to learn about your business, and understand how the logo fits into your overall brand.

The Business Card

The Ubiquitous Business Card now comes in two flavors: Regular and Virtual.

We are all familiar with the traditional business card printed on quality paper stock with your contact info, logo, tagline, and maybe something extra. Some are printed on clear plastic, some are little squares, occasionally, some are edible, though I don't see what good that does.

The Virtual card is something new. It lives on your smart phone, meaning you can share it by texting, emailing, or just touching a prospect's smartphone and, just like that, they have all your pertinent info read into their address book. You can have several versions of your card with different designs for different purposes.

Think of it as a mini press kit or PR hack you don't have to feed.

The addition of a QR code, (short for Quick Response code) is an array of black and white squares or pixels set in a grid that stores data, like your website URL. A potential customer can scan the QR code and have instant access to your website.

This is the single most important piece of business communicati you can have. All the necessary info about your company in an easy-to-carry format. Keep several of them handy at all times. Treat them like seeds, and plant as many of them as possible.

Sundry Pieces of Collateral

To the chagrin of printers and the delight of trees, the need for sending out expensive printed pieces has diminished, thanks once again to the Internet. That said, a supply of brochures, fliers, and postcards are handy tools to use while networking or making sales calls. Since they encapsulate your business, they can save you the trouble of having to endlessly repeat yourself— this is especially handy after too many white wine spritzers.

Merchandise, pens, t-shirts, baseball caps, and other fun stuff to give away are useful in keeping your name literally in front of people's faces. As a networking veteran, I haven't had to buy a coffee mug or pen in decades.

That's pretty much it for the basics, now it's time to face the world and let people know that you're out there. In the next chapter, we'll delve into the world of Digital Marketing.

QUIZ
Choose the Correct
Course of Action:

Circle the best answer:

Why is Branding important?
A. The bigger you look, the more you can charge.
B. It makes it easy to tell which livestock belongs to you
C. Advertising people need the money
D. It establishes your identity and sets you apart from the competition.

Which of these are Branding Archetypes?
A. Sneezy, Doc, and Bashful
B. Groucho, Chico, and Harpo
A. Hero, Caregiver, Rebel
D. Butcher, Baker, Insurance Adjuster

What does USP stand for?
A. Unique Sales Proposition
B. Unlimited Sucky Problems
C. Unilateral Self Propulsion
D. Unnecessary Stuff Propagated

Why find your Why?
A. Because
B. People buy why you do something before they buy what you do.
C. Without why you can't know what's what or who's who, and you're nowhere
D. If you don't find it, who will?

123

Chapter 12:

Digital Marketing

Here, there, and everywhere

The internet has created a level playing field, giving small businesses (that's you) equal access to potential customers anywhere, anytime.

Consumers have access to more information about products and services than ever before, making them really picky. Your target market wants to get to know you before they decide to do business with you. They want authenticity and are not impressed by the usual hype.

As marketing guru and obsessive blogger Seth Godin has said, **"Marketing used to be about the things you make, today it's about the stories you tell."**

Potential customers want to know, your values, how you can help them meet their needs, what happens behind the scenes, and what you have in common with them.

Your internet presence is the place to tell your stor.

It All Starts With Content

Of course, all those internet pages would be boring if you had nothing to put on them. You'll need what we call Content. Content can be any information that informs, entertains, educates, or inspires your target audience. It can take the form of words, photos, videos, graphics, illustrations, slide shows, or any combination thereof.

There are two essential requirements of Content:

• It has to be relevant to your business and your target audience. If people visit your website for plumbing supplies, they're probably not interested in your thoughts on the decline of the music industry.

• It has to be interesting, or at least not dull. With attention spans shrinking and the amount of information growing, you need to hold people's attention. You can't assume that your visitors will hang around to read every word just because you have up-to-date and even necessary information.

Know your Audience.

Write for them and not just to extoll the virtues of You, Inc. It is helpful to put myself in the shoes/sandals/footwear of my customers. Why are they reaching out to me? What are they looking for? What are their needs as it pertains to my business, and the type of services can I offer? (I'm a digital marketing professional. If they need anything else, say spiritual guidance, they'll need to look elsewhere. I always wish them well.)

Think of Content creation as an extension of the sales call. What questions do potential clients/customers usually ask you? What are the essential points of your sales pitch? All of those are great starting points.

Content does not have to be limited to stuff you create yourself. The web has a time-honored tradition of Sharing or Curating content — repurposing information you may have found on news sites, other people's blogs, social media pages, or stuff overheard on the way to work. You're fine as long as you appropriately attribute the source of the info and give credit where it's due.

126

Websites, Social Media, and the Great and Powerful Google

All Marketing has become Digital Marketing. With Google, and to a lesser extent Yahoo and Bing, being the first place everyone goes to find everything, having a comprehensive online presence is essential.

Website

Your website is the center of your marketing universe! It's your turf on the internet, the one place where anyone on planet Earth can find information about you and your business. It allows you to establish and maintain your brand identity, communicate with your customers, and happily sell, sell, sell.

It's also the only place on the internet that you control—all those Social Media and third-party sites belong to someone else, as anyone who's had to cope with Facebook's surprise interface changes or Google's algorhythms can tell you.

An essential business website should include the following:

- **Logo and Branding Elements**: Establishes your identity
- **Homepage:** Grabs the users' attention, sets the tone
- **Company Information:** Background, capabilities, anything to establish credibility
- **Case Histories or Examples of your Work:** Establishes your credibility in your area of expertise.
- **Photos and Video:** Show your business in the "Real World."
- **Contact Information:** How can prospects reach you?

Social Media

After the Internet, nothing else has radically changed the way businesses interact with their markets than social media. If traditional advertising can be considered a monologue, then social media would be a conversation, actually many conversations about many subjects happening all at once. You'll know exactly what I mean if you've ever attended an Italian family dinner on any given Sunday.

Social media allows businesses to engage with their target markets and vice-versa on many levels. It's creating a relationship where the customers/users generate the content, interact with each other, and share reviews, complaints, images, and videos.

The platforms provide Analytics on how your visitors have interacted with your pages. You can see what kind of traffic your post generated and how many Likes, Shares, and Comments each post received. This will show you what content did or did not resonate with your audience.

This information is particularly valuable if you decide to fork over some bucks and buy advertising, referred to as paid media. Paid media allows you to use that data to target your ads to specific audiences. Check the individual platforms for advertising options.

Each social media site has its own purpose.

Facebook

Still the mothership and the largest social media site out there. If it were a country, it would be the 4th largest in the world—behind China, Russia, and India. Its sheer size demands that you maintain a presence there. You should create a separate business page so you don't have to explain those hot tub photos to your clients. You can also purchase highly targeted ads at reasonable rates.

X or the platform formerly known as Twitter

There has been much upheaval due to the change of ownership. You should monitor the platform to see if your customers are still on it and if you agree with any changes in its tone. That said, the basics of Twitter have stayed the same. Twitter is the source of business news and information. Aside from sharing tweets and posting your sudden insights, you can Direct Message any of your followers, a most effective way to reach members of the media.

LinkedIn

Facebook for business. The preferred site for job recruiters and seekers is another excellent way to connect with companies and business people. As with all social media sites, the key is to be active and build a reputation or a following! LinkedIn is also working on becoming a source for business content and has added a blogging feature for all you would-be thought leaders out there.

YouTube

Google purchased YouTube a few years ago, and it (YouTube) is now the second most visited site after Facebook. (Google + YouTube would be the largest). Since Google owns it, placing your video content on YouTube, as opposed to uploading it to your hosting account, earns you points with the big G and does wonders for your search engine rankings.

Pinterest

At first glance, it's a virtual scrapbook, pictures of stuff that people, mostly women, find interesting or entertaining. A closer look will reveal an interactive community that is very effective for e-commerce: becoming an online catalog. It's also useful for group projects; I know several people who have used it for wedding planning.

Instagram

Once famous for photos of food and complaints about foamless cappuccino, it has grown to be a legitimate source of news, information, and where to find delicious gazpacho. They've recently added video and are tinkering with some advertising models, so it's increasingly becoming an effective marketing tool.

TikToc

TikTok is the trendy, relatively new kid on the block. It is a social media app dedicated to short-form videos created for and consumed by users. The average maximum lenght is three minutes. The format lends itself to entertainment and comedy. However, it is increasingly used for infotainment. Some users even become social media celebrities.

Blogging

You have an enormous advantage internet-wise if you can write or coerce someone to write for you. Blogging gives you a chance to get your thoughts, insights, and opinions out there and be recognized as that ultimate of all internet stars, "A Thought

Leader"— making you a thinker of thoughts others are thoughtfully thinking about, I think. If you're ambitious, consider guest blogging on other blogs for additional exposure and credibility.

If you get a big enough following, you can call yourself an "Influencer," See below.

Email Marketing

The one thing you cannot do is overtly sell. While most sites will accept paid advertising to some extent, using the social space to "hard sell" is not only frowned upon but will get you unfriended, unfollowed, and generally unofficially "blacklisted." The key is to create relationships, build trust, and become a contributing member of whatever community you join, and when people need what you're selling, they will find you.

Mobile Marketing

Everybody accesses the internet via smartphones, and some bypass the internet altogether by texting and using apps. Mobile marketing promises or threatens, depending on your point of view, to change the game once again, with textingreplacing email in some circles.

Mobile marketing brings a level of immediacy no one has ever seen before, literally putting your business in the palm of your client's hands. Just look at the variety of Apps now available. While still reasonably expensive, if you look around on the web, there are App Options to fit most budgets if you want to get in on the game.

Influencers

Influencers are social media stars with a large and loyal following and can "influence" their fans to buy, try, and use products and services. Sometimes it works; sometimes, it doesn't. Companies in Healthcare, Fashion and Beauty, Travel and Lifestyle—even Technology can benefit from having an internet celeb post, tweet, or TikTok about them.

QUIZ
Choose the Correct
Course of Action:

True or False:

_____ Marketing used to be about what you make, now it's about what you make- up.

_____ Good Content has to be interesting and relevant to the reader

_____ You don't need a website unless you live in 1998.

_____ No one really understands Social Media, so forget about it.

_____ If Facebook were a country, it would be the Netherlands after a long weekend.

_____ Twitter is 240 characters of trouble.

_____ LinkedIn is best if you're all about business.

_____ TapeWorm, Stethoscope, and BluberryHoliday are all names of social media platforms.

_____ Mobile marketing means having a sign on top of your car.

_____ The best marketing plan in the world is a talkative friend who's an obsessive networker.

Chapter 13:

Networking Events

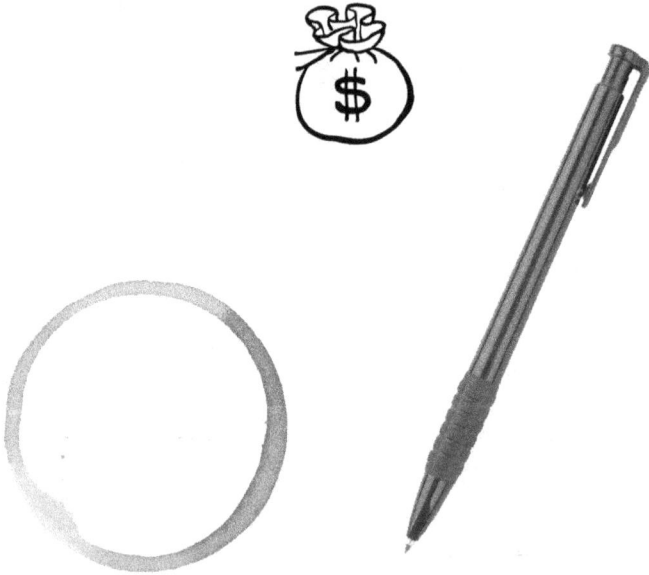

Shake hands with your income stream

Networking is essential to the start of any new enterprise. Making connections online is very effective, but nothing beats going out there and meeting your potential customers/ clients face to face, mano a mano, and cocktail to cocktail.

Whereas they used to be excused for going out for a drink, the modern networking event is part singles bar, part new business pitch, and a part scavenger hunt. It combines the best and worst of all three: excitement, focused communication, and a "look what I found" optimism.

Like all forms of social communication, there are certain unwritten rules of behavior. After decades of consuming oceans of free drinks and gallons of onion dip, I have ascertained the following "Rules of the Networking Road."

Networking is Not Selling

Nobody goes to a networking event because they have a $25K project burning a hole in their pocket. People generally go to get work, not give it. There is nothing more annoying than introducing yourself to someone only to have to stand there and listen to a 10- minute pitch on Financial Planning—or the time I simply said, "Excuse me," to a corporate-looking type as I was trying to get to the bar and found myself getting a lecture about mold in my basement.

The next worst thing is to actually ask someone for work. It's both an awkward situation and annoying. I once paid about $250 for a table at a trade show. I had my promo material prominently displayed and was happily answering questions about my business. During a lull, a guy approached my booth, launched into his pitch, and asked if he could be my accountant. I replied that if he gave ME the $250 I shelled out for the table, I would be glad to stand there and listen to anything he had to say.

Networking events are best seen as laying the groundwork for future success. I like to think of it as planting seeds. You are looking for people with whom you might build long- term, steady, productive relationships.

Hmmm, what else does that remind you of?

How Networking is Like Dating

Of course, there have been periods in my life where networking was dating. I tried to come away with opportunities for getting either sex or money—but enough about me.

As with dating, in networking, you are searching for that perfect stranger with whom you will form a deep, long-lasting, and, in this case, profitable relationship. Not too much pressure.

To improve your odds, I've broken the types of people you might encounter at a networking event down to the following four "Networking Archetypes":

The Hunter/Gatherer

These people are all business and extremely focused. No small talk, no little hot dogs, one drink that gets nursed to death. They are the Delta Force of networking, there to "hunt" prospects and "gather" business. As you are talking, they are mentally calculating how much you are costing them if you do not turn into a humungousclient. However, if you do have something they want/need, they could turn into YOUR humungous client.

The Party Guy/Gal

It would be nice if they got some business out of this, but they're really here to have a good time. Lots 'a jokes, anecdotes, and friends. They talk, they talk incessantly, they talk to the point where you never get a chance to say anything. And despite all that talking, you have no clue as to what it is they do! But many a business deal has started as a night out, and no matter what happens, you'll have a good time at least.

The Mommy/Daddy

They just want to help. They're interested in every aspect of your life, even though they didn't know you existed until you entered the room and put on your name tag. They will ask about your kids, your dog, and your mother; if you don't have a dog, they know where you can get one. In fact, they will offer to get you anything you may be lacking since they know just about everybody. If you can wade through all that nurturing, they may even know your next client.

The Watcher

They see all, they know all, they're also invisible. They don't network so much as they bear witness, mentally cataloging all that passes before them but hardly interacting. Unless you look really hard, you wouldn't even know they were there, and since they have the world on a "Need-to-Know" basis, talking to one is like interrogating a terrorist suspect.

However, when you find one who is comfortable enough to open up to you, you will find a wealth of information and contacts. Just watch what you tell them, they remember everything!

Where to Find Networking Opportunities

Networking opportunities are everywhere and nowhere. Lunch with a business associate or two or three is a networking opportunity. So are family gatherings, trips to the store, high school reunions, and even funerals.

For a larger pool of like-minded networkers, it's best to join groups, associations, clubs—almost anything that lets you regularly get together with people of similar interests.

Usually, membership in one group will create opportunities in another, as many will hold joint events.

Venues should be crowded enough to meet enough new people but not so crowded that you're trapped in a corner. Generally speaking, these events are held in one of two locations: a Bar/Restaurant or an Event Room. Event Rooms can be stuffy and somewhat confining, though the crowd is usually more focused on doing business.

Bars and Restaurants are more fun, but people might be there more for the drinks and snacks than to widen their networks. If you're having no success at all, I recommend you hang out by the kitchen and catch the hors d'oeuvres as they come out from the kitchen.

You can usually tell the type of people expected to attend an event by the food that's passed around. Shrimp means you've got a high-class crowd; raw veggies and a preponderance of Chicken Sate means no one special; Pigs in a Blanket means they're there to have fun!

To network anywhere, always have a stack of business cards with you, and remember, no selling! Networking, especially in an informal setting, is more about starting relationships. Instead of just talking, ask questions and get to know the other attendees.

Networking Kabuki

Networking done well is an art, a blend of movement and conversation—sort of like a ballet with name tags.

136

The Entrance

As with any public event, it's important to make a proper entrance. Get there on time. Get there too early, and they'll think you're setting up tables and placing chairs. Get there too late, and the little hot dogs will be gone. Try to pre-register whenever possible. Usually, you'll get an "early bird" discount, but more importantly, you'll get a cool pre-printed name tag in a plastic holder. Otherwise, you'll be given one of those name tags with a sticky back that doesn't stick to anything for long, and you'll have to write in your name with a leaky marker. Not all that cool.

Once you enter, size up the room. See anyone you know? Anyone you'd like to know? Most importantly, where's the bar?

The Drink

Next to the Business card, the Drink is your most important prop. People just look cooler holding a drink. It tells people you are engaged, that you're a player. With your preprinted name tag hanging around your neck, you're ready for action.

What you drink isn't all that important. Wine, beer, mixed drink, soda, water, just don't get plastered, and don't use a straw. It's hard to look like a dynamic Captain of Industry while sucking on a piece of plastic. You might as well be wearing one of those handwritten name tags.

The Approach

Once you're set, it's time to "get busy." I often walk around the entire room once, seeing who's there, and getting a feel for the place. When I'm ready, I find it best to jump in, so I usually start with the person nearest me, making eye contact, holding out my hand in that "Hey, let's shake hands" manner people often do, and saying something clever like, "Hi!, I'm Michael."

I then ask the person what's the nature of their business, tell them what I do, and take it from there. Another technique is standing with a small group until someone notices you. I don't time it, but I try to keep it to 5 minutes or so, do the business card exchange, and move on. The idea is to connect with as many people and collect as

137

many business cards as possible, so keep the encounters short.

You may find yourself embroiled in a never-ending conversation. The important thing is not to panic. You can either excuse yourself because you need another drink, or need to use the restroom. I usually say something like "Great meeting you. I'm going to mingle." and quickly move on. If you meet someone you'd like to get to know better, well, you have their card.

The Business Card (VIRTUAL BIZ CARDS)

Not having enough business cards with you is like showing up naked. Though getting cards rather than giving them is more important, not having one to give in return breaks the social contract of networking.

Business cards aren't going to do you any good sitting in a drawer or in your pocket or bag. Be generous with them and spread them around. Keep in mind that looks can be deceiving. That nerdy guy or plain gal may have a successful business that needs your services, or they may have a capability that will allow you to land a big account.

After the Event: The Follow-up

It's essential that you follow up with everyone you made contact with. especially with anyone you think might have some potential. Email is best. Include your website address (No website? Did you crawl out of a cave to attend this event? Get thee to a developer!). Offer to get together again to continue whatever discussion you may have initiated in the first meeting. Usually people who answer and agree to meet again are promising prospects.

After that, it's a matter of finding an appropriate project or situation. Sometimes these embryonic relationships grow into clients. Sometimes they grow into semi- partnerships. Sometimes you make a friend to take to the next event.

Frequency is the key. If nothing happens, no biggie. There's another networking event next week!

QUIZ
Choose the Correct Course of Action:

Networking Types: Match the Type to the description
- Hunter/Gatherer
- The Watcher
- The Mommy/Daddy
- The Party Guy/Gal

Hangs out in the corner, taking notes they'll never use

Treats Networking events like they're on Safari, you feel like an Antelope at a watering hole

Shows you a good time but has no business to speak of

Only wants to talk about you and your needs; they have no life

Networking Kabuki: Match the Component to the description
- The Drink
- The Approach
- The Entrance
- The Follow-up

Something to do with your hands
The reason you collected all those business cards
Recovering attorneys. What do you do?
Stride confidently into the room, quickly look around, and find the bar ASAP.

Chapter 14:

Thoughts on Money

Invoices, investors, magical thinking

To some, it makes the world go 'round. To others, it's the root of all evil. To most, it's life's report card.

Money is, in many ways, the whole point of running your own business. All of the reasons for working for yourself: self-determination, inner peace, that sense of fulfillment, all hinge on being able to pay your bills, put food on the table, and have enough left over for the occasional luxury like a European vacation or a major medical procedure.

If you need practical information, there are countless books, articles, blogs, webinars, and pamphlets that will gleefully advise, lecture, cajole, assess, explain, and warn you about what you should, should have, should not, or should not have done, with your money.

What I can do, however, is speak from personal experience and, for what it's worth, offer a few key observations.

Lesson #1 If it ain't broke

But taking a hard-nosed, bottom-line approach to your business can cause problems. Back in college, I had a part-time job as a file clerk in a mid- sized accounting firm. Many of their clients were in the garment industry, people who had literally started with a push cart—they couldn't even afford horses—and had grown their businesses to the point where they now employ hundreds, if not thousands, of people.

Being responsible adults, they sent their children to big-time business schools so that they could keep things running when the old man retired. Upon taking the reins, the kids started running the shops "like businesses" and instituted all sorts of procedures, protocols, practices, and things in writing.

The old men had built their empires on handshakes and personal relationships, things that were lost when the new regime was put into place. As you might have guessed, without those relationships, the businesses suffered. On the bright side, they improved accounting services, which meant they could accurately record things as they went down the tubes.

Beware Investors Bearing Gifts or "Come into My Parlor," Said the Venture Capitalist to the Unsuspecting and Trusting Entrepreneur.

You may, from time to time, find that you're coming up short and that you could benefit from an infusion of cash. You might even be offered a couple of bucks by a well-meaning friend, a friend of a friend, or a generous local Mafioso. "What's the harm," you ask, "many businesses are started, or at least get a boost, from investor money."

The issue is control, and you may find that the investment dough comes with more strings than a yo-yo factory.

At first, your benefactor might appear to be a willing partner, maybe even a savior, as they offer such reassuring words as:

"We believe in you. We're in this for the long haul. Success doesn't

142

happen overnight." "We're willing to be patient because we want to do this right."

and the ever-popular,

"You're the one calling the shots. You'll retain total control of your company."

In short, they promise to give your little acorn of a company the time it needs to grow into the mighty oak of positive ROI (Return On Investment). After all, they believe in you and share your vision, and, gosh darn it, you're all in this together!

But—as soon as that check clears, the clock starts ticking. In my experience, the "Goldilocks period" (not too hands-on, not too hands-off, but just right) lasts about six months—a year if you're lucky. One day, just as you're getting comfortable, "Take your time, we're all friends" turns into "We're shutting you down, thank you for playing" as they pull the plug on your dream, rip out your heart and tell you to have a nice day.

You may have started your business to pursue your dream, but investors invest to make a profit. As a result, they can be short-sighted, impatient and decide that they'd rather put their money somewhere else. I have seen several clients and friends go under because their investors lost patience and things weren't progressing fast enough.

Allow me to illustrate:

Dots All, Folks!

During the "dot com" boom of the late 1990s and early 00s, Venture Capitalists freely lavished millions of dollars on anyone who could write the word "Internet" on a napkin. No idea was too outlandish, too far-fetched, or too expensive. While few of these companies were turning a profit at that time, they were inventing the future and teaching the world a new way to do business.

The turning point came with the sale of the media giant Time Warner to America Online

—it was as if a little girl with a lemonade stand had swallowed the Coca-Cola Company. Panic ensued as we entered the financial Twilight Zone, and overnight all that talk about "It's a great big beautiful tomorrow" turned into, "Show me my money." Funding was pulled, loans were called in, and the dot com boom became the dot com bust just as the industry was about to blossom.

Needless to say, they were a bit premature in proclaiming that "there's no way to make money on the internet."

Taking a Bite Out of a Cookie Company

CR is a nice young man who inexplicably developed a passion for baking cookies. He slowly grew his business over a couple of years, introducing new flavors every few months. Then, one Christmas season, he had an opportunity to sell his wares in holiday gift baskets at a Midtown Manhattan pop-up store.

There was, of course, a catch. He needed cash to rent and decorate the space, move his inventory, and hire "a hot cookie"' to work the crowd. As luck would have it, a wealthy friend offered to advance him the money. Yes, it was a significant amount of "dough," but this was a sure thing—those cookies were going to fly off the shelves.

As usual, things did not go as planned. After the holidays, the "friend" wanted his investment back, and the cookie business crumbled.

"Silent" Partners

Aside from being a member of what a friend of mine used to refer to as "The Sperm Club" (those lucky enough to inherit their money or have access to a family fortune), there is a way you can finance your business with partners who will give you complete autonomy, and who will never pull the rug out from under you.

I am, of course, talking about Visa, Master Card, Discover, and American Express. They will never question the validity of your strategy or your management ability as long as you make those monthly payments.

Invoicing, Determining Your Fee or "Do You Have a Budget for This Job? Well, of Course, You Don't..."

Estimating what to charge for your product or service is the trickiest part of working for yourself. Ask for too much, and you might not get the business, ask for too little, and you might as well call it a hobby. There are many sources of information on the subject that offer various formulas for determining what you should be charging, something like:

Your Time + Expenses + What You Need to Pay Other People to get the job done + Taxes + Lunch Money + An Aggravation Surcharge if the Client/Customer is a Bozo = Your Ideal Fee.

If only life were that simple.

The fact is that most clients/customers are reluctant to tell you how much they want to or can spend—it usually comes down to as little as possible. You'll end up charging what you can get. At the same time, you don't want to be bidding against yourself by volunteering to lower your price. No matter how low you go, there is always some dolt who will do the job for less.

I have three scenarios illustrating a different billing conundrums :

Adjusting the Scope of Work to Match the Fee.

I'm not in business to turn down work, especially during a "dry spell." When faced with a client with a small budget, you can still do business if you adjust the amount of work to match their budget.

As a point of reference, I use the 1930's Marx Brother's classic, *Monkey Business*. Chico is trying to convince a gangster to hire Harpo and him as bodyguards. Before committing, the gangster wants some indication of just how effective the two would be, resulting in the following negotiation:

Chico: "You pay a little bit, we little bit tough; you pay very much, we very much tough; you pay too much, we too much tough."

Gangster: "I'll pay you plenty."

Chico: "Then we plenty tough" They shake on it, sealing the deal.

Even the Greats Had to Negotiate

Sometimes it may be worth your while to accept less than the job is worth, so you'll have a "really nice sample" or experience that you can use to justify more considerable fees down the road. When Michelangelo first accepted the contract to paint the Sistine Chapel, he was just supposed to paint portraits of the Twelve Apostles. But, as we know, he soon had a grander vision.

As depicted in *The Agony and the Ecstasy*, Michelangelo presented his revised sketches to Pope Julius II on a battlefield in Italy. (Pope's acted a bit differently in those days.) Then, talking over the sounds of cannon fire, the two start quibbling over the adjusted fee— it went something like this:

Pope: "It's genius."

Michelangelo: "Thank you, Your Holiness. Holy Father, it is much more work . . ."

Pope: "What are we paying you now?"

Michelangelo: "3,000 Ducats, Your Holiness"

Pope: "It's worth 10. I can only pay you 6."

Michelangelo, grudgingly: "Thank you, Your Holiness."

Ever the perfectionist, the Sistine Chapel was his idea of a "really promo piece." Michelangelo took four years to finish painting his masterpiece. The Pope was so exasperated that halfway through, he threatened to hire a young man, Raphael, to finish the job. As with today, there's never enough money to do it right the first time, but there's always money to do it over.

Negotiating Against Yourself

One thing I have learned is that the issues remain the same regardless of the size of the job—it's only a matter of scale. In this case, the issue is trying to get a feel for how far the other party is willing to go—you could wind up cutting your price prematurely.

Andrew Carnegie's U.S. Steel dominated the industry in the late 19th Century. So when Carnegie decided to retire to a life of philanthropy, his competitors retained J.P. Morgan to negotiate the buyout deal. The two men met through intermediaries and finally negotiated a deal for $480,000,000 (roughly $13,086,197,802.20 today). "You are the richest man in the world," Morgan told Carnegie once they had concluded their business.

Sometime later, their paths crossed again, and Carnegie mused that he should have asked for another $100,000,000.

"You would have gotten it," replied Morgan. Of course, we'll never know if he was telling the truth, but I get the feeling J.P. was busting some half-a-billion-dollar balls.

Magical Thinking

Every new business starts with a leap of faith—that you can do something better than the next guy or gal and convince others to pay you handsomely. This may or may not be true, but you never know until you put your ideas into action.

Regardless of what you tell other people, it's imperative that you remain realistic with yourself as far as money is concerned. Financially speaking, that leap of faith can become a headlong dive into an empty swimming pool if you fully buy into your hype, especially if you are "buying in" with your own money—real or imagined.

Magical Thinking is an outgrowth of the "if I build it, they will come" mentality. That any idea you have is so fantastic, new, and compelling that customers will throw money at you once they see it. How can anyone say no? They won't be able to help themselves.

It's believing that if you want something strong enough, it will appear before you.

Most of us realized this approach to life doesn't work in High School, right around the time we were trying to find a date for the Prom. Unfortunately, some never get the message.

147

I once worked with a bombastic individual who was in what can be called Merchandising. He had one of the most unique companies I'd ever seen. He created specialty, branded clocks, and watches for large corporations and organizations. His clients included companies like Mercedes Benz, L.L. Bean, the National Hockey League, to name a few.

As impressive as that might sound, he also suffered from an overabundance of self- confidence and an even bigger sense of optimism. Yet, despite those major accounts, his success was undermined by his Magical Thinking.

I had the opportunity to go on several new business pitches with him, and every time a prospective customer would say something like, "That's interesting, let me get back to you." he would hear, "We have a deal, where do I send the incredibly large check."

To make matters worse, he would start spending as though he already had the potential new account and, more importantly, their money in hand.

As a result, he was always broke—the more success he had (or thought he had), the deeper in debt he'd become. This set up a financial death spiral of needing to close more businesses to get out of debt, only to get deeper in debt because he spent more of the money he thought he had. Finally, it got to the point where he couldn't afford any new business. The cost of success was higher than the cost of failure.

Marriage to a beautiful woman who also happened to be an accountant—all that self- confidence could be very seductive — finally straigtened hm out.

QUIZ
Choose the Correct
Course of Action:

Be wary of investors because . . .

____ They can pull their money at a moment's notice.

____ They forget about you, and you'll have to chase them down to pay them back

____ Require too much paperwork

When is the best time to ask the Pope for money?

____ During a battle

____ During lunch

____ During the Inquisition

____ During a strange interlude

When negotiating with J.P. Morgan, you should . . .?

____ Dont say you wish you had a nose that big full of nickels.

____ Ask for the moon, then add another 100 million.

____ Have a steel empire you're looking to unload .

____ Wear spats.

Magical Thinking is . . .

____ Something required of all Disney employees

____ Something taught at Hogwarts.

____ Something fatal to your bottom line, a toxic mixture of overconfidence and optimism

____ Something that just became legal in Denver

Chapter 15:

Everything Else

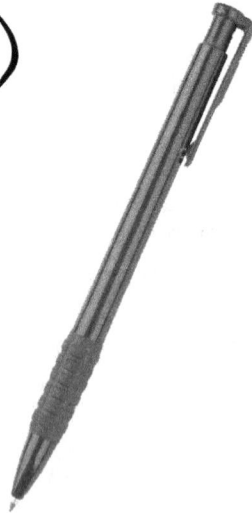

Your life outside of your buisness.

There's more to your life than running a business! Deciding to be your own boss is as much a lifestyle choice as it is a career decision.

If you merely change jobs, your commute will be altered, your office mates will take some getting used to, and you'll have to find another place to get your morning bagel and coffee—but there's still a commute, office mates, and a nearby deli.

"Going out on your own" means just that—you're out there, on your own, all by yourself—and you'll be dedicating enormous amounts of time and energy to your new enterprise. Unfortunately, most embryonic entrepreneurs fail to consider how this affects the other aspects of their lives.

Circumstances beyond your control may cause you to put off things like parking tickets, seeing friends, eating regular meals, vacations, and major surgeries. That's fine in the short term, but soon things will catch up with you making your life resemble a multi-car pileup of threatening letters, damaged relationships, and, very possibly, scurvy.

This is the great paradox. You started a business to have more control over your professional life, only to find that you may have less control over your personal one. Here are a few of the ramifications, good and bad, I've had to deal with since becoming the "CEO of Me."

Issue #1

The Ripple Effect of Cash Flow Issues

I start every month with the best of intentions. Still, occasionally I'll have a series of late invoices or a stretch where one or more clients have not paid me on time, and I find myself screening phone calls, weighing which bills I have to pay now and which ones I can pay later, or just generally being terrified of the mail man.

Disruptions to the flow of cash can lead to all sorts of misunderstandings with the powers that be. A late payment here or there will eventually cause problems. But, as I have learned, running afoul of the IRS, the Department of Motor Vehicles, or any major Credit Card companies can halt your entrepreneurial express faster than an anvil on a train track.

The IRS

Yes, we know your ultimate goal as a business owner is to be so successful that you can avoid paying taxes altogether. However, until that happy day, I advise you to pay close attention to due dates, payment schedules, letters, notices, postcards, and other forms of communication from any tax collecting entity you are beholding to.

Like a needy friend, they will try anything to get your attention. Ignore them at your peril; they are tenacious, but their patience is limited.

And nothing says, "Where the hell have you been," like a tax levy.

If you're lucky not to know what a tax levy is, it's waking up one morning and finding out that all your checks have bounced. Panic-stricken, you run to the bank to find that one of the aforementioned tax-collecting entities has finally gotten tired of not hearing from you and, in a playful moment, has frozen all your assets.

On the bright side, all they want is what is due them. I have had tax levies removed within hours once I've either paid up or informed them about my situation. If you are responsive and honest about why you might not have paid, they are more than willing to work with you, extend deadlines, and arrange payment plans. Yes, you may encounter additional fees and penalties, but you'll do so from the comfort of your home and not from some minimum-security facility.

The Department of Motor Vehicles

The easiest way to get on the wrong side of the DMV is to avoid paying your parking tickets. Not only will fees and penalties accrue quickly, but in some cases, they are not content to wait. Unlike the IRS, the DMV will strike without warning, "booting" your car, suspending your license, or just towing your vehicle away (NOTE: Booting is the practice of placing a large orange collar around one of your tires, it immobilizes your care and screams "Dead Beat" to anyone passing by.)

I discovered how playful the DMV could be on one balmy summer evening. Walking to my car after a night out in Manhattan, I arrived at the block where I had parked to find— nothing. My car was gone. I called a passing patrol car to report the "theft," but once I gave them a year, make, and model of my car (a 1996 Nissan Maxima), I was assured that "No one would ever steal THAT car," and that it had most likely been towed.

Many phone calls later, I discovered that the City Marshal had towed it for unpaid parking tickets. All they would tell me was that my car was "at an undisclosed location" and that if I ever wanted to see it again, I had to bring the amount due, IN CASH, to one of the more obscure parts of Brooklyn (something like Avenue M, an area so out-of- the-way that apparently, the streets don't have names, just letters).

All that was missing was the instruction to put the cash in a plain paper bag and leave it under a park bench. I gathered up the money, and a friend drove me to what turned out to be a fortified storefront with thick walls and even thicker glass partitions. I paid the attendant, who then revealed the "undisclosed location" was on the other side of Brooklyn—at an old Army depot.

Before leaving, I asked for a receipt. As he handed me a bad photocopy of my proof of payment, he suggested that I leave it on my dashboard for the next six months because they don't update their records all that often—and all this can happen again.

Credit Card Companies

Credit card companies are somewhere between the cold hand of the DMV and the relentless though collaborative nature of the IRS. They are still intent on taking your money, and they can be very nice about it, but their ability to remember a past slight rivals that of my Sicilian grandmother.

They will call you when your account is past due and cheerfully assist you in updating it. But, during a credit crunch, they can become the financial equivalent of Hannibal Lecter.

I found this out during an anniversary trip to Las Vegas, where my wife and I were renewing our vows at an "Elvis Wedding." After several days of merriment, I was informed that my credit card had been declined when I attempted to settle the hotel bill. I was surprised because I had made sure my account was current before leaving home.

The credit card company in question had cut my credit limit to the bone because I had been a tad late in the past—my tardiness made me a "bad risk"—though I had soon paid all I owed. In addition, the reduction of credit had placed a black mark next to my name in the book of life. My credit references have sent potential lenders recoiling in horror at the sight of my Social Security number.

Oh, they're still polite and cheerful when we speak, but, as with an old lover—the unspoken sentiment is just below the surface—you disappointed us once, and we'll never let you do that again.

Bad credit is the result of late payments, no payments, or keeping an outstanding balance on your account for too long. There are companies, too numerous to name here but only a Google search away, who can help with credit repair and you get back in their good graces.

Issue #2 Family and Friends:

Understandable misunderstandings

No other area of my life has been affected more than that of my personal relationships. Family and friends may need some time to adjust to your new reality, dealing with the unpredictable work schedule, the inevitable money problems, and the emotional ups and downs that come with the entrepreneurial territory.

In addition, it's all too easy to develop a bunker mentality. You start to feel isolated, lose touch with the world, and become weird. Since I do not have a stable of co-workers, I have found that my non-business relationships are much more important to me. If everyone I speak to is a client or a vendor, all my human interactions are reduced to transactions—like the Moonlight Bunny Ranch but without the happy endings.

Family

No group of people has been more mystified, critical, and, at times, more supportive of my efforts than those nearest and dearest to me. My family's reactions have swung wildly from pride to bewilderment, sympathy to impatience, and awe to ridicule, all within one conversation.

My Mother seems to think I am in some semi-retirement—like her friend's son, Vinnie. He's also "home a lot" due to a "work-related disability." But, as I have explained countless times, there is a big difference between "being at home" and "working from home." I may be working in my pajamas, but I am WORKING—with clients and deadlines and billing—just like grownups.

Because my time appears too unstructured, I get the occasional list of chores and requests, "Since you're home, can you . . . " bring the clothes to the dry cleaners, take the dog to the vet, buy something for dinner, pick up the kids, pick up the dry cleaning, fix the ceiling fan, paint the kitchen, take mom to the doctor, pick the dog up from the vet, cook dinner, and so on. Many conference calls have been cut short because a chicken was about to burn in the oven.

Friends—In Real Life and Online

The great philosopher and TV personality Soupy Sales (Google him, if you must), would close his show by telling us kids, "Be grateful for your friends because, without them, you're a stranger."

As I wrote previously, the Covid pandemic changed the nature of personal relationships and spawned what one could call "Zoom Culture," since direct, face-to- face meeting with other humans was kept to a minimum. We communicated and lived through our technology, visiting people remotely, ordering food or relying on Amazon to deliver the basic and not-so-basic necessities of life to our door— and then run away from the door before we could open it and say hello.

I enjoy talking with people in different lines of work. Zoom culture made that both easier and harder at the same time. I met people I would never have from around the world, while my relationships with family and friends who lived close by suffered from a self-imposed distance.

I have spent my professional life as a graphic designer/art director— my cohorts tend to be the types who obsess over minutia. I have sat through many a mind-numbing conversation over the relative merits of too much or too little letter spacing.

People from different walks of life give me a fresh perspective on the world, perspectives that can add another dimension to my work. The problem is getting together—lunches, dinners, and drinks all get moved around the calendar with depressing regularity. I have several friends I only see twice a year because it can take six months for our schedules to be in sync. To that end, connecting with friends online is a viable option. I have reconnected with several old friends virtually and rekindled several relationships.

Pets

Decker is an eight-pound black toy poodle with a serious attitude. When I work at home, he is as close as I got to have an office colleague —staying with me as I worked, listening to my ideas, sharing lunch, and generally acting as the unofficial concierge. No one got within half a block of the place without being "announced." I learned plenty from the little guy—see the chapter on Client Management.

Children

Being able to rearrange your schedule to be there for your children is one of the significant advantages of being your own boss.

The fact that you have the flexibility to be available for their most important moments is a significant perk. I have been there for all of my daughter's milestones, from birth to first words and steps, to first days of school, assemblies, graduations, and a variety of the usual childhood emergencies.

I have helped with homework, built dioramas, edited science projects, and attended parent-teacher conferences. Despite seeing one or two student plays I could have done without, it's all been well worth it.

Issue #3

Taking care of yourself because, without you, you're nothing.

Finally, we end up where we began, with you and your belief in yourself. You started this journey as a way to better yourself. If you are like me, you'll begin by caring for everyone and everything before tending to your needs. Bad idea—you'll soon be well on your way to being the worst boss you've ever had, and, aside from an out-of-body experience, there is no way to quit yourself.

The phrase "if you've got your health, you've got everything" should have been coined by an entrepreneur. Regardless of what your balance sheet might say, your business is only as healthy as you are. It once took me forty-five minutes to write a two-line email because

I refused to give in to an impending bout of the flu. I finally realized that I'm just not as clever as I think I am when I'm on antihistamines.

Keeping in Shape: Eating, Sleeping, Exercising

Think of yourself as an entrepreneurial athlete, a self-employed ninja, or a warrior with a smartphone. But, like all of those alpha male stereotypes, you need to be in peak physical shape to handle clients, an increased workload, and stay awake during those tedious 2-hour phone/Zoom conferences.

In the heat of battle, I have begun many a day skipping breakfast, having a late lunch, and something like cheese doodles for dinner while putting in a 36-hour day, only to crash for the next day, or two, or many. Whatever extra time I have gained by not taking care of myself, was offset by the time it's taken me to recover.

It's important to realize when it's time to stop. Eventually, you'll smack into the dreaded Law of Diminishing Returns—the more you work, the less you get done. Best to walk away and pick up where you left off once you've recharged.

Hobbies & Non-Business Related Activities

Sometimes it's not a matter of sleep. It's a matter of using a different part of your brain or just getting away from work and doing something you enjoy. Hiking, biking, stamp collecting, line dancing, getting wasted with a group of friends, or having a quiet moment with a loved one or loved one to be—if all you do is work, you'll go stale and resent your boss (that's you, by the way). In this sense, finding time for yourself to enjoy life is a business decision.

Try to pick an activity that is very different from your business—as the following chart illustrates:

Expertise	Hobby
Finance	Art, Karaoke, Talking to a toddler, Shopping
Insurance	Hiking, Oragami, Doing other people's taxes
Contractor	Cooking, Flower arranging, Hanging out in bad neighborhoods
Plumber	Ballroom dancing, Stamp collecting, Ant farms

I leave you with some words of wisdom from Fennel Hudson, author of *Fennel's Journal*. Written by outdoorsman & traditional angler Nigel 'Fennel' Hudson, the *Fennel's Journal* series of books is for anyone who enjoys time outdoors in quiet natural surroundings, escaping the pressures of life and traditional things.

"The speed of modern life is an oppressive thing, and the corporate world is quick to punish those with an honest heart. Qualities such as 'nice, honest, kind, happy, relaxed, sincere, innocent' are frowned upon as weaknesses.

Yet these values are the essence of a good person. Unfortunately, they can be lost like sand through your fingers if you don't keep the balance."

The happier and healthier you are, the better you will perform (and the more money you'll make), and aren't those the reasons you went out on your own in the first place?

Epilogue

Ok, that's all I've got, time for you to go for it.

"Far better is it to dare mighty things, to win glorious triumphs, even though checkered by failure than to rank with those poor spirits who neither enjoy nor suffer much because they live in a gray twilight that knows not victory nor defeat."
-Theodore Roosevelt

Herein lies the distillation of my experiences and insights from almost three decades of being my own boss. As I wrote in the Introduction, most books about starting your own business are written by former corporate executives with access to venture capital and an address book full of influential contacts. This book is not intended for them— they don't need me, this book, or anyone else. Their success is practically assured.

I wrote this book for the everybody else. Those who have been laid off, left behind, forgotten, taken for granted, or retired too early. Those who have a dream and a belief that we can do better for ourselves than others can do for them.

Go ye forth, my brothers and sisters, dream big, fail miserably, succeed wildly, take your shot and leave nothing on the table, build your life your way, and change the world. Win or lose, you'll be better for it.

Someone has to get lucky—it might as well be you.

Resources

Information at Your Fingertips

I have provided lists of useful software, apps, websites, and information throughout this book. Rather than have you fumble through the pages in search of something you thought you might have read, I've collected those practical pieces of wisdom in this easy-to-use-appendix.

- **Small Business Resources**

- **Finding Freelance Help**

- **Top Business Apps**

- **Project Management Software**

- **Home Office Computer Requirements**

- **How Chat GPT Can Help Grow Your Businesses**

Small Business Resources

Small businesses often require various resources to thrive and succeed. Here are some essential resources that can benefit small businesses:

Small Business Administration (SBA): The SBA offers a wide range of resources for small businesses, including loans, grants, business counseling, and assistance with government contracts. Their website provides access to valuable information and tools.

SCORE: A nonprofit organization that provides mentoring services and free business advice to small businesses. Their volunteers, comprised of experienced business professionals, can offer guidance on various aspects of running a business.

Small Business Development Centers (SBDCs): Small Business Development Centers (SBDCs): SBDCs are partnerships between the government, colleges, and universities. They provide free or low-cost consulting and training services to small businesses, assisting with business planning, marketing, financial analysis, and more.

Business incubators and accelerators: These organizations provide support, mentorship, networking opportunities, and sometimes even physical office space to startups and small businesses. They often have specific industry focuses and can help companies to grow and scale.

Online resources and communities: Numerous online platforms and communities cater to small businesses. Examples include the Small Business section on the U.S. Chamber of Commerce website, business forums such as Reddit's r/smallbusiness, and industry-specific online communities where entrepreneurs can seek advice, share experiences, and connect with others.

Small business grants and competitions: Many organizations and government agencies offer grants or host competitions to support small businesses. These grants and competitions can provide funding, recognition, and exposure. Keep an eye out for opportunities relevant to your industry or location.

Trade associations and industry-specific resources: Joining trade associations related to your industry can provide access to valuable resources, networking opportunities, industry research, and advocacy. These associations often offer educational events, conferences, and publications tailored to their members' needs.

Remember to consider your specific business needs and goals when exploring these resources. Adapting and leveraging the resources that align with your industry, business model, and stage of growth is essential.

Finding Freelance Help

1. Fiverr 1. Fiverr —Fiverr is an online marketplace that connects freelancers offering digital services in 500+ categories.to people or businesses looking to hire. *See fiverr.com*

2. Toptal— An exclusive network of the world's top freelance software developers, designers, finance experts, product managers, and project managers. *See toptal.com*

3. Freelancer.com—The World's most significant freelance marketplace. *See freelancer.com*

4. Upwork—The largest network of independent professionals and get things done—from quick turnarounds to significant transformations. *See upwork.com*

 5. Guru—Create your free job posting and receive Quotes within hours. Find and hire expert freelancers. Compare the Quotes you receive and hire the best freelance professionals. *See guru.com*

Top Business Apps

One way to spend money to save or "make time" is through technology. There are many job-specific apps, software packages, and third-party platforms (and more coming daily) that you can access on an as-need basis to make your work life more efficient and your life-life easier. Many offer a free seven to thirty-day trial, after which there will be a small monthly fee, but you can cancel your subscription as soon as it's no longer helpful.

Some of the more popular third-party platforms are also available as Apps, so you can download them to your mobile device and have them with you everywhere, all the time:

1. Microsoft 365 — With Word, Excel, and PowerPoint in one app, Microsoft 365 is the destination for creating and editing documents on the fly. – www.microsoft.com/en-us/microsoft-365/what-is-Microsoft-365

2. Amazon Web Services — Build, Deploy, and Manage Websites, Apps, or Processes on AWS' Secure, Reliable Network. Sign Up for a Free Account - aws.amazon.com/

3. Google Workspace —Get access to business versions of Google Meet, Chat, Drive, Docs, Sheets, and more.- workspace.google.com/

4. Zoom — I mentioned Zoom in a previous chapter. It's a video conferencing website/ platform that makes it possible to meet and work with anyone, anywhere. zoom.us/

5. Slack — If you are working with teams, Slack is an instant messaging program where you can share messages, announcements, documents, audio, and video clips and keep everyone on the same page, https://slack.com/

6. Grammarly — A super spellcheck, Grammarly catch spelling, grammar, punctuation, clarity, and engagement errors while allowing users to customize their style, tone, and context-specific language.- https://grammarly.com/

7. Canva — A free-to-use online graphic design tool. Use it to create social media posts, presentations, videos, logos, and more.

8. Trello—A Collaboration/Project Management tool. Trello is a visual tool that empowers your team to manage any project, workflow, or task tracking. Add files, checklists, or even automation: Customize it all for how your team works best.

9. Gusto — An innovative payroll software designed to automate and streamline the payroll process for small to medium-sized businesses. With its user-friendly interface and powerful features, Gusto Payroll helps business owners save time, reduce errors, and comply with tax regulations.

10. Wave — Online bookkeeping with many free options; Wave allows you to search transactions, design accounting reports and reconcile data across other Wave products. Plus, you can calculate sales tax automatically, customize payment terms and enjoy access to easy-to-understand cash flow insights.

11. Squarespace — An all-in-one content management system, or CMS. With a single subscription, you can make a website, host your content, register your custom domain name, sell products, track your site's analytics, and more.

12. Constant Contact —Email marketing software that primarily helps businesses create and track branded emails, websites, online stores, and more in one online marketing platform

13. QuickBooks — QuickBooks is a user-friendly, simple accounting software that tracks your business income and expenses and organizes your financial information, eliminating manual data entry.

14. Storage Options—Once you've created all thet niffty suff, you're going to want too keep it where you get your hands on it, or better yet, pass it on to some one else. The two best options I have found are **Dropbox** and **Google Drive**. Both allow you to set up folders, access and share those folder with designated team members from anywhere and buy more space as you need it. Bye, bye flash drives

Project Management Software

1. monday.com is a Work Operating System (Work OS) designed to help teams work without limits regarding project and task management. Monday work management offers a user-friendly and intuitive interface with a range of customizable features that cater to any team's specific collaboration and communication needs across industries.

2. Trello is a web-based project management tool that uses a board-based approach to help individuals and teams organize their tasks and projects. It is a popular and user-friendly tool that allows users to easily track their progress, collaborate with team members, and visualize their workflow intuitively.

3. Basecamp is a project management tool that helps teams to stay organized, collaborate efficiently, and complete projects on time. It was first launched in 2004 by 37Signals but later rebranded as Basecamp in 2014. Basecamp is a cloud-based project management software accessed through a web browser, desktop, or mobile application.

4. Wrike is a cloud-based project management software designed to help teams streamline workflows and collaborate more effectively. It was founded in 2006 by Andrew Filev and has since grown into a popular tool used by businesses of all sizes to manage projects from start to finish.

5. Asana is a popular project management tool designed to help teams collaborate and manage their tasks and projects more efficiently. Asana has gained a reputation as a reliable and easy-to-use tool for project management, and many businesses and organizations worldwide use it.

Do a Google search for whatever you need (video conversion, for instance), and you'll be surprised at what you find.

Home Office Computer Requirements

1. Increased processing power: Ensure your desktop/laptop/ mobile device has enough advanced processing power to handle complex tasks and significant amounts of data with incredible speed and efficiency. Intel Core i5 or i7 or AMD Ryzen 5 or 7 are good options. You should also have enough memory.

2. Cloud computing: The rise of cloud computing has enabled businesses to store their data and software in offsite data centers, reducing the need for on-site servers and storage. This has also made it easier for employees to access data and applications from any location and device.

3. Improved security: With the increasing cyber-attack threat, security has become a significant concern for businesses. Advances in cybersecurity technologies, such as advanced firewalls, intrusion detection systems, and encryption technologies, have helped to protect against threats and keep sensitive data safe.

4. Collaboration and communication tools: Today, all computers have WiFi installed for remote work, and collaboration has become essential for businesses. Advances in video conferencing, messaging, and project management software have made it easier for teams to communicate and work together from anywhere in the world.

5. Mobile computing: The increasing power and portability of laptops, tablets, and smartphones have enabled employees to work from anywhere. This has led to greater flexibility and productivity in the workplace. Some of these have touchscreens that eliminate the need for a stylus. Others are hybrids between a desktop and a tablet — a docking station allows your tablet to act as a desktop with a separate keyboard.

6. Security and Support: Look for a computer with built-in security features like antivirus software, firewalls, and encryption capabilities. You can add additional security from any number of software vendors. Warranty and Support: Choose a computer from a reputable manufacturer with a good warranty and technical support options if you need assistance.

Using Chat GPT for Small Businesses

AI can benefit small and new businesses by automating several tasks, freeing you to grow your business.

It's important to note that while AI can offer significant advantages, small businesses should carefully consider their specific needs, budget, and the level of expertise required to implement and maintain AI systems. Working with AI experts or leveraging user-friendly AI platforms can make it easier for small businesses to adopt and benefit from AI technologies.

Personalization: AI algorithms can analyze customer data and behavior to provide personalized recommendations, offers, and content. This level of personalization helps businesses tailor their marketing efforts to individual customers, improving customer satisfaction and boosting sales.

Data Analysis: AI algorithms can process and analyze large amounts of data quickly and efficiently. Small businesses can leverage AI to gain insights from customer data, market trends, and internal operations. This information can be used to make data-driven decisions, optimize operations, and identify growth opportunities.

Automation: AI can automate repetitive and time-consuming tasks, freeing up valuable time for small business owners and employees. Tasks such as data entry, inventory management, and social media posting can be automated, allowing staff to focus on more strategic and value-added activities.

Predictive analytics: AI algorithms can analyze historical data and identify patterns to make predictions and forecasts. Small businesses can use this capability to anticipate demand, optimize inventory levels, and plan their resources more effectively.

Competitive analysis: AI-powered tools can gather and analyze data about competitors, market trends, and consumer preferences. This information can help small businesses identify gaps in the market, track competitor strategies, and adjust their offerings accordingly.

Financial management: AI can assist with expense tracking, cash flow management, and budgeting. AI-powered tools can automate financial processes, provide real-time insights into financial health, and help small businesses make informed financial decisions. Chat GPT can also be a valuable tool for sales-related tasks:

Lead generation: Chat GPT can engage with potential customers and collect information to generate leads. By interacting with website visitors or through messaging platforms, Chat GPT can ask qualifying questions, provide product information, and capture contact details. The sales team can use this data to follow up with leads and convert them into customers.

Customer inquiries: Chat GPT can handle customer inquiries and provide real-time support. It can answer questions about products, pricing, availability, and shipping options. By providing prompt and accurate information, Chat GPT can enhance the customer experience and help decision-making, ultimately increasing the chances of a sale.

Customer support: Chat GPT can handle customer inquiries and provide support 24/7. Small businesses may need more resources to offer round-the-clock customer service, but Chat GPT can bridge that gap by responding instantly to common customer questions. This improves customer satisfaction and ensures that queries are addressed promptly.Chat GPT can also handle objections and provide relevant information to address customer concerns.

Upselling and cross-selling: Chat GPT can identify opportunities for upselling or cross-selling by understanding customer needs and preferences. It can suggest complementary products or services, highlight bundle offers, or recommend upgrades to increase the average order value and maximize sales revenue.

Sales analytics: By analyzing interactions with customers, Chat GPT can provide insights into customer preferences, frequently asked questions and common pain points. This information can help businesses identify trends, optimize sales strategies, and improve the effectiveness of their sales processes.

Financial management: AI can assist with expense tracking, cash flow management, and budgeting. AI-powered tools can automate financial processes, provide real-time insights into financial health, and help small businesses make informed financial decisions. Chat GPT can also be a valuable tool for sales-related tasks:

Lead generation: Chat GPT can engage with potential customers and collect information to generate leads. By interacting with website visitors or through messaging platforms, Chat GPT can ask qualifying questions, provide product information, and capture contact details. The sales team can use this data to follow up with leads and convert them into customers.

Customer inquiries: Chat GPT can handle customer inquiries and provide real-time support. It can answer questions about products, pricing, availability, and shipping options. By providing prompt and accurate information, Chat GPT can enhance the customer experience and help decision-making, ultimately increasing the chances of a sale.

Customer support: Chat GPT can handle customer inquiries and provide support 24/7. Small businesses may need more resources to offer round-the-clock customer service, but Chat GPT can bridge that gap by responding instantly to common customer questions. This improves customer satisfaction and ensures that queries are addressed promptly.Chat GPT can also handle objections and provide relevant information to address customer concerns.

Upselling and cross-selling: Chat GPT can identify opportunities for upselling or cross-selling by understanding customer needs and preferences. It can suggest complementary products or services, highlight bundle offers, or recommend upgrades to increase the average order value and maximize sales revenue.

Sales analytics: By analyzing interactions with customers, Chat GPT can provide insights into customer preferences, frequently asked questions and common pain points. This information can help businesses identify trends, optimize sales strategies, and improve the effectiveness of their sales processes.

Product recommendations: Chat GPT can suggest suitable products or services based on customer information. By analyzing customer preferences, past purchases, and browsing behavior, Chat GPT can offer personalized recommendations. This level of customization can lead to higher conversion rates and customer satisfaction.

Sales assistance: Chat GPT can act as a virtual sales assistant by guiding customers through the sales process. It can provide information about product features, compare different options, and offer additional incentives or discounts to encourage purchases.

Before running through the streets yelling that the machines are taking over, remember that Chat GPT is only the first AI system readily available to the general public. Others are already embedded in your everyday life, such as the voice recognition that powers Alexus and Siri. so at least give it a try. If you do find AI helpful in running your business, start keeping up with the latest developments.

And finally, the most powerfull, useful, significant buisness resource ever invented:

Google!

Besides getting directions and finding restaurant reservations, it has countless business uses. For example, I use it to troubleshoot software/hardware/appliance issues. It is easier to use than any manual. It's also a quick and easy spell checker. Anytime I'm stuck, I find something on Google to get me moving again.

In addition, Google provides you with a suite of software tools, starting with Google Docs, an online word processor that is included as part of the free, web-based Google Docs Editors suite, which also includes Google Sheets, Google Slides, Google Drawings, Google Forms, and Google Sites. The best part is that since they are web-based, you can access them and your work from any computer with an internet connection.

You Oughta Be In Business

About the Author

Artist, designer, digital pioneer, teacher, entrepreneur, and author Michael Pilla has spent his life at the crossroads of art, technology, and withering sarcasm.

Born and bred in the Bronx, NY, he graduated from Pratt Institute and worked as a designer and then art director. During the dot-com boom, he held creative leadership positions at iVillage.com and ModemMedia, designing interactive advertising for Fortune 500 companies. After the inevitable downsizing, he formed Pilla Creative Marketing, bringing the power of the Internet to start-up and small businesses.

Michael shares his wisdom and experience by conducting seminars and webinars on digital marketing and has taught Internet and design courses at local colleges. You can read more about marketing issues on his blog PillaTalks.com

Michael Pilla supporting Bob-O's Cheesesteak Truck,
a small business in New Jersey

www.ingramcontent.com/pod-product-compliance
Lightning Source LLC
Chambersburg PA
CBHW060601200326
41521CB00007B/632